New Testament Studies

VI

THE ORIGIN OF THE NEW TESTAMENT

AND THE

MOST IMPORTANT CONSEQUENCES OF THE NEW CREATION

BY

ADOLF VON HARNACK

TRANSLATED BY

THE REV. J. R. WILKINSON, M.A.

FORMERLY SCHOLAR OF WORCESTER COLLEGE, OXFORD
AND RECTOR OF WINFORD

Wipf & Stock
PUBLISHERS
Eugene, Oregon

Wipf and Stock Publishers
199 West 8th Avenue, Suite 3
Eugene, Oregon 97401

The Origin of the New Testament
and the most important consequences of the new creation
By Harnack, Adolf
ISBN: 1-59244-591-8
Publication date 3/17/2004
Previously published by Williams and Norgate, 1925

PREFACE

THE purpose of the following pages will be fulfilled if they serve to forward and complete the work accomplished by the histories of the Canon of the New Testament that already exist. The history of the New Testament is here only given up to the beginning of the third century; for at that time the New Canon was firmly established both in idea and form, and it acquired all the consequences of an unalterable entity. The changes which it still underwent, however important they were from the point of view of the extent and unification of the Canon, have had no consequences worth mentioning in connection with the history of the Church and of dogma. It is therefore appropriate, in the interests of clear thought, to treat the history of the Canon of the New Testament in two divisions; in the first division to describe the *Origin of the New Testament*, in the second its *enlargement*. Moreover, it is necessary—though this is a point that hitherto has been seldom taken into account—that the consequences that at once resulted from the new creation should receive due consideration as well as its causes and motives. For the origin of the New Testament is not a problem in the history of literature like the origin of the separate books of the Canon, but a problem of the history of cultus and dogma in the Church.

A. v. H.

BERLIN, 22*nd May* 1914.

CONTENTS

APPENDICES

INTRODUCTION

THE collection of writings *Apostolic* and Catholic (the New Testament), the *Apostolic* Rule of Faith, the *Apostolic* character assigned to the Bishops (dependent upon succession) mark the chief results of the inner development of Church history during the first two centuries. This conclusion, as modern text-books of the history of Church and dogma show, is to-day almost universally accepted. And yet, with all our excellent treatises on the history of the origin of the New Testament, and in spite of the far-reaching agreement of our scholars in just this province of research, it is still not superfluous to show how clearly and comprehensively the history of the Primitive Church has manifested itself in the leading principle, in the creation and compilation of the New Testament, and how vast and decisive, and, on the other hand, how various and even contradictory were the consequences of its appearance.[1] Moreover, the question whether

[1] In my *Lehrbuch der Dogmengeschichte* (1^4, S. 372–399) I have given a sketch of the history of the origin of the New Testament from the standpoint of the history of Dogma. The object of the following pages is to give a more comprehensive and clear-cut

and to what extent the New Testament was consciously created has not yet been cleared up. Lastly, though it is firmly established that this collection of inspired writings is a remainder-product—for once upon a time everything that a Christian wrote for edification counted as inspired—yet there is still need of more rigorous investigation of the circumstances which necessarily led to restriction and choice.

discussion of the chief points in the story of the development, and of the motive forces at work, in connection with the general history of the Church, and to state more forcibly the consequences of the creation of the New Testament.

THE ORIGIN OF THE NEW TESTAMENT

I

The Needs and Motive Forces that led to the Creation of the New Testament

If the trained observer surveys merely the Title and the Table of Contents of the New Testament, whether in its present form or in the older and shorter form of the close of the second century, and if he adopts the viewpoint of the Apostolic Age, he is faced by at least five great historical problems.

The Books of the New Testament
(or the New Testament).

The Gospel
- according to Matthew.
- according to Mark.
- according to Luke.
- according to John.

The Apostolus
- The Acts of the Apostles.
- Thirteen Epistles of Paul.
- The Epistle of Jude.
- The 1st and 2nd Epistles of John.[1]

[1] These two epistles have the testimony of the Murat. Fragment and of the Corpus Cypr. (In Tert., *De Pudic.*, " in primore " is to be read in place of " in priore epistola [Joannis] ").

The Apostolus {
(The 1st Epistle of Peter).
The Revelation of John.
(The Revelation of Peter).
(The Shepherd of Hermas).[1]

The five problems are these :—

1. What is the reason and how did it come about that a second authoritative collection of books

[1] The three bracketed works have a special history. In regard to 1 Peter it is not quite certain whether it belongs to the earliest form of the New Testament. The two Apocalypses may indeed be assigned to the most ancient form, but they were objected to at once, and this in the community of Rome, which, as we shall show, was probably the very birthplace of the New Testament. The opposition to the Revelation of Peter was at first the weaker of the two, but it very soon and completely attained its object, while in the case of the Shepherd of Hermas it was strong from the beginning but did not find complete success until later. In the earliest (Roman) list of Canonical Scriptures which we possess, mention is also made of a "Wisdom" of Solomon which we are told was composed by Christian admirers of Solomon. Probably "Jesus Sirach" is meant, which was also called "Ecclesiasticus." We have here a singular phenomenon which we cannot quite comprehend. From the standpoint of the close of the second century no special importance need be assigned to the order of the Gospels nor to the position of the Catholic Epistles (*Philastr.*, 88: "Septem epistulæ Actibus Apostolorum conjunctæ sunt") which could also be placed before the Pauline Epistles. Only the precedence of the Gospels before all the rest of the writings and the placing of the Acts of the Apostles at the head of the second division in idea and soon in actual practice (Murat. Fragment, see also Irenæus and Tertullian) are firmly established. But it would be a mistake to imagine that at the end of the second century absolutely no interest was taken in the question of the number and order of canonical writings. The contrary is proved by the petition of the brother Onesimus to Melito, Bishop of Sardis, that he would give him information concerning the number and order of the books of the Old Testament. Melito responded to this request, and by a method of counting of his own set the number at twenty-one (Euseb., *H.E.*, iv. 26, 13).

arose among Christians? Why were they not satisfied with the Old Testament, or with a Christian edition of the Old Testament, or—if they must needs have a new collection—why did they not reject the old? Why did they take upon themselves the burden and complication of two collections? Finally, when did the idea of a fixed second collection first appear?

2. Why does the New Testament contain other works in addition to the Gospels, and thus appear as a whole with two divisions (Gospel and Apostle)?

3. Why does the New Testament contain four gospels and not one only?

4. Why could only one "Revelation" keep its place in the New Testament? Why not several or none at all?

5. Was the New Testament created consciously? How did the Churches arrive at one common New Testament, seeing that the individual communities, or provincial Churches, were independent, and that the Church was one only in idea?

From the standpoint of the Apostolic Epoch these five questions appear as just so many enormous paradoxes so long as one does not go deeply beneath the surface of events as they developed. I purpose to attempt a brief discussion of these questions; and it would be perhaps much to the point if future works on the history of the Canon of the New Testament started in the same way.

§ 1. *How did the Church arrive at a second authoritative Canon in addition to the Old Testament?*

From the standpoint of the Apostolic Epoch it would be perfectly intelligible if the Church, in regard to written authorities, had decided to be satisfied with the possession of the Old Testament. I need not trouble to prove this. We should, however, have been to a certain extent prepared if, as time went on, the Church had added some other writings to this book to which it held fast. Indeed, in the first century, even among the Jews, the Old Testament was not yet quite rigidly closed, its third division was still in a somewhat fluid condition, and, above all, in the Dispersion, among the Greek-speaking Jews, side by side with the Scriptures of the Palestinian collection, there were in circulation numerous sacred writings in Greek of which a considerable number became gradually and quite naturally attached to the authoritative collection. It would therefore have been in no sense surprising, nor would it have been regarded as extraordinary, if from the Christian side some new edifying works had been added to this collection. This actually happened here and there with Apocalypses; indeed, attempts were even made to smuggle new chapters and verses into some of the ancient books of the Canon.[1] In this fashion

[1] See my *Altchristl. Lit.-Gesch.*, 1, S. 849 ff.; ii. 1, S. 560–589; *Texte u. Unters.*, Bd. 39, Hft. 1, S. 69 ff. That round about the

Christians might have proceeded in yet bolder style, without doing anything unusual, and so might have been able to satisfy requirements which were not met, or not completely met, by the Old Testament. Lastly, judging from the standpoint of the Apostolic Age, we should not have been surprised if in the near future the Old Testament had been rejected or set aside by the Gentile Churches. When the word had gone forth that one should know nothing else than Christ Crucified and Risen, when it was taught that the Law was abolished and that all had become new, the step was very near to recognise the Gospel of Christ, and nothing else. "I believe nothing that I do not find in the Gospel" (Ignat., *Phil.*, 8)—what object then was served by the Old Testament? That the Apostle who taught all this nevertheless himself accepted the Old Testament offered no special difficulty. Gentile Christians knew very well that the Apostle, who to Jews became a Jew, for his own person and out of regard to the Jews, had clung to many things that were not meant to be accepted by others or need no longer be accepted. For all these possibilities (the Old Testament alone; an enriched Old Testament; no Old Testament) we should thus have been prepared; but we should have been absolutely unprepared for that which actually happened—a second authoritative collection.

year A.D. 200 Tertullian wished to add Enoch to the Old Testament is well known, and the reasons he gives are very instructive. See *Sitzungsber.*, 1914, S. 310 f.

d this come about ? It is true indeed that ct that an Old Testament existed had the important part in the suggestion and creation New Testament; and yet for decades of years Old Testament was the greatest hindrance to ch a creation, more especially because the Old Testament in a very complete and masterly way was subjected to Christian interpretation,[1] and so Christians already possessed in it a foundation document for that new thing which they had experienced. Still, far down beneath the movements of the time, a more sure preparation was being made for that which was to come, namely the New Testament, than for all the other possibilities. These had their strength in forces which lay on the surface; but under the surface a new spirit was working from the beginning, and was striving to come to light.

Here three questions present themselves: (*A*) What motives led to the creation of the New Testament ? (*B*) Whence came the authority that was necessary for such a creation ? (*C*) Supposing the necessity of a New Testament, how did it actually come into being ?

(*A*) Here a series of motives increasing in importance were at work; but it was the last of these that demanded a new *written* authority *side by side*

[1] St Paul himself offered a rich collection of such Christian interpretations, although he, as a rule, allowed to the Law its literal sense.

with the Old Testament (and this without abandonment of the same).

(1) The earliest motive force, one that had been at work from the beginning of the Apostolic Age, was the supreme reverence in which the words and teaching of Christ Jesus were held. I have purposely used the expression "supreme reverence," for in the ideas of those days inspiration and authority had their degrees. Not only were the spirits of the prophets subject to the prophets, but there were recognised degrees of higher and highest in their utterances. Now there can be no doubt that for the circle of disciples the Word of Jesus represented the highest degree. He Himself had often introduced His message with the words "I am come" (*i.e.* to do something which had not yet been done), or, "But I say unto you" (in opposition to something that had been hitherto said). This claim received its complete recognition among the disciples in the unswerving conviction that the words and directions of Jesus formed the supreme rule of life. Thus side by side with the writings of the Old Testament appeared the Word of "the Lord," and not only so, but in the formula *αἱ γραφαὶ καὶ ὁ κύριος*[1] the two terms were not

[1] (The Scriptures and the Lord.) I cannot be persuaded that "the Lord" as a title of Jesus was first conceived on Gentile-Christian soil. The idea of "Messiah" simply includes that of "Lord." The formula "The Scriptures and the Lord" has manifold attestation direct as well as indirect in the Apostolic and post-Apostolic epoch.

only of equal authority, but the second unwritten term received a stronger accent than the first that had literary form. We may therefore say that *in this formula we have the nucleus of the New Testament.* But even in the Apostolic Age and among the Palestinian communities it had become interchangeable with the formula *αἱ γραφαὶ καὶ τὸ εὐαγγέλιον*[1]; for in the "Good News" was comprised what the Messiah had said, taught, and revealed.[2] These two almost identical formulæ, though they do not as yet distinguish the followers of Jesus from ideal Judaism, nevertheless mark a breach with Judaism as it actually existed.[3]

[1] (The Scriptures and the Gospel.)

[2] It is a waste of time to discuss which of the two formulæ, *αἱ γραφαὶ καὶ ὁ κύριος* or *αἱ γραφαὶ καὶ τὸ εὐαγγέλιον*, is the earlier. Concerning "evangelium" and the earliest history of the conception, I refer to my book *Entstehung und Entwickelung der Kirchenverfassung* (1910), S. 199-239, especially S. 224 ff.

[3] We must cry halt for a moment, for the historian of the New Testament in order to gain a more exact conception of what actually happened must survey what might have happened. If the motive here described could have had free course, undisturbed by other motives, we should have expected that a collection of authoritative sayings of Jesus loosely compiled or in more connected form, and at the most enriched by some eschatological elements, would have taken its place beside the Old Testament. And for a time this is what actually happened both in the case of the looser and more connected forms. *In the compilation Q that lies behind the Gospels of St Matthew and St Luke we have an example of the looser form, and in the Christian version of "The Two Ways" of the more connected form.* The latter work, in the form which it has received in the "Didache," is especially interesting, because in it an attempt is made to base not only the ethics but also the most important institutions of the Christian communities (such as Baptism, Prayer, Fasting, the Eucharist, the rules of life, etc.) upon sayings of Jesus, and thus

(2) The second motive, manifested with peculiar force in St Paul, but by no means exclusively in him, is the interest in the Death and Resurrection of the Messiah Jesus, an interest which necessarily led to the assigning of supreme importance to, and to the crystallisation of the tradition of, the critical moments of His history. Under the influence of this motive "the Gospel" came to mean the good news of the Divine plan of Salvation, proclaimed by the prophets, and now accomplished through the Death and Resurrection of Christ;[1] and it would be

to give the whole Christian position an "evangelical" foundation, so that it should not depend on the Old Testament as its sole *written* authority. Lastly, this ancient Didache, in so far as it claims to be both "Teaching of the Lord" and "Teaching of the Apostles," (Διδαχὴ κυρίου διὰ τῶν ιβ' ἀποστόλων) also implies that relative identification of Christ and the Apostles which, as we shall see, was the most essential condition of the origin of the New Testament. Thus without exaggeration we may say that Q (*in its earliest form*), *as well as the old Didache, aim in their own fashion at being a New Testament or "the New Testament.*" It was not outside the limits of possibility that Christendom should have produced as its "New Testament," nothing except a work like the "Didache" side by side with the Old Testament (and the Gospels). How nearly this happened we may judge from the important fact that, even after the New Testament was created, the production of works like the Didache, based upon the authority of the Lord and the Apostles (Constitutions, Canons, etc.), continued up to the fifth and sixth centuries. *The motive which led to this authoritative literature is thus older than those which led to the New Testament.* When we take up works like the "Apostolic Canons" we should remember that we are dealing with rivals of the New Testament, in idea more ancient and venerable than the New Testament itself, in spite of their wild and audacious development of that idea.

[1] A change also takes place in the concept of ὁ κύριος. In this term Christ is now regarded from the point of view of His nature and acts rather than as the teacher divinely commissioned.

felt that an account of the critical moments of the life of Christ must take its place side by side with the Old Testament history regarded as prophetic.[1] Then at once there must have arisen among Christians the desire and endeavour to prove the concordance of prophecy and fulfilment in order to establish their own faith and confute the unbelief of the Jews. Thus the Church had just as much need of an historical tradition concerning Jesus as of the Old Testament; and a comparison point by point of prophecy and fulfilment was also an absolute requisite. These requirements were still covered by the formula *αἱ γραφαὶ καὶ ὁ κύριος* (or *τὸ εὐαγγέλιον*), but the concept *ὁ κύριος* (*τὸ εὐαγγέλιον*) demanded now, in addition to the moral (and eschatological) sayings of Jesus, an historical record. *With this stage of development correspond our Gospels, or rather the many Gospels of which St Luke still speaks.* That

[1] The scope of the record to which this feeling led was at first purely arbitrary. The plan of the Markan Gospel shows most clearly that the chief interest lay in the Story of the Death and Resurrection. If the teaching of Christ was to be combined with this story it was necessary to give some kind of preliminary history. This is what St Mark gives. But what he gives is to the very smallest extent determined by interest in the fulfilment of prophecy—simply because the material to hand was so insignificant in this respect (yet see what St Matthew tries to do with it). It was not until courage was found to pass from this preliminary history (the story of our Lord's teaching and wonderful works) to what we to-day call "preliminary history" (Matt. i.–ii.; Luke i., ii., etc.) that the scheme, "Fulfilled Prophecy," could be so forcibly applied, as it was already in the story of the Death and Resurrection, and then for the most part to facts that happened because they were wanted.

they were many in itself proves not only the acuteness of the need for them, but also the carelessness that prevailed in the matter of authenticity. It was not the author's authority that at first carried these writings, but their own content. By the historical element of this literature the separation between the Churches and the Synagogue was set in yet stronger relief than by the Didache literature; for the latter could still connect with Jewish ethic, and was as a matter of fact developed from it (*cf.* "The Two Ways"), whereas the historical literature laid emphasis upon everything that was to the Jews a "scandalon," and thus established and widened the cleft between them and the Christian bodies. Under the influence of the second motive, together with the first, the formula "The Holy Scriptures and the Lord" was transformed into "*The Holy Scriptures and the* (*written Gospels*) *or the* (*written*) *Gospel*,"[1] The historical situation in the Churches that corresponded to this new formula was that which preceded the creation of the New Testament.[2]

[1] Accordingly the Gospels were also called "The Scriptures of the Lord": see Dionysius Cor. (c. A.D. 170) in Euseb., *H.E.*, iv. 23, 22 (Clem. Alex. and Tertullian).

[2] Here also it is well to halt for a moment. If the above mentioned motive together with the first had had free course, without any interference from new motives, the result must have been as follows: either a written gospel (like our Gospels) would have taken its place beside the Old Testament with all the dignity which its content afforded or, on the other hand, a compilation of concordances of Old Testament prophecies and events in the history of Jesus (together with some work like *Q* or like the Didache). The first alternative,

(3) The third motive belongs quite essentially to St Paul and to those who learned from him. It

as is well known, came into being. The Jewish-Christian Churches, *as long as they lasted,* added *one* written gospel, the "Gospel of the Hebrews," or the "Gospel of the Ebionites," to the Old Testament, and *nothing else.* It is also conceivable that the Egyptian Churches during part of their history had only a Gospel in addition to the Old Testament. It is, moreover, certain that many important Churches for about half a century (*c.* 130–170 or 180) set one Gospel (perhaps several—we need not discuss this at present) beside the Old Testament, and that in the Syrian and Arabian Churches this state of affairs lasted *until the middle of the third century.* We are here concerned only with establishing these facts. Whether these Gospels were valued for their content only, or whether form and the authority of the author were already of importance, and what was the exact relation in which they stood to the Old Testament—these also are questions which lie for the moment outside our scope. In any case it is clear that it was not only not outside the limits of possibility, but that the circumstances rather suggested that a permanent "New Testament" should have arisen comprising only a Gospel (one or several). It is possible to ask whether the course of the Church's history would not have been simpler if she had kept to a Gospel or to the Gospels as her "New Testament." But would not the Old Testament have been too strong in the Church if she had been obliged to dispense with the Pauline Epistles? To ask the question means to answer it in the affirmative. The Johannine Gospel could not have performed the absolutely necessary service that the canonised Paul has performed for the Church—still less St Mark or St Luke. As for the second possibility that instead of our Gospels and the Pauline Epistles we should have received only a compilation of concordances between prophecies and fulfilments (with or without *Q*)—here, too, there is no lack of attempts in this direction. Such compilations existed as is shown by the works of Justin when compared with other works (from the Acts of the Apostles onwards). Note especially the Ἐκλογαί of Melito (Euseb., *H.E.*, iv. 26, 13 f.), unfortunately lost to us; it was made up of "extracts from the Law and the Prophets concerning the Saviour and our whole Faith." There was no small danger that Christians should have remained satisfied with such concordances, and that development on these lines would have resulted in a cramped and finds expression in such words as these: "Christ is the end of the Law," "The Law is given by Moses, Grace and Truth came through Jesus Christ," and the like. Pauline Christians, and many that were not Pauline, were convinced that what Christ had brought with Him, in spite of its connection with the Old Testament, was something "new" and formed a "New Covenant." The conception of the "New Covenant" necessarily suggested the need of something of *the nature of a document;* for what is a covenant without its document? An enthusiast like Ignatius could indeed exclaim: 'Εμοὶ ἀρχεῖά ἐστιν Ιησοῦς Χριστός, τὰ ἄθικτα ἀρχεῖα ὁ σταυρὸς αὐτοῦ καὶ ὁ θάνατος καὶ ἡ ἀνάστασις αὐτοῦ,[1] but the quite exaggerated paradox of the statement of itself teaches us that it could never become common property. No; if the handwriting that was against us is torn in pieces then there must be a new handwriting which is for us! If the written Law is abolished then the written Grace and Truth must appear in its place. And yet we notice that at first neither

superficial New Testament. Fortunately, however, none was skilful enough to find a satisfactory form for this conception. Hence it has always remained *formless* in the Church; and, so far as I can see, it is owing to this fact that from this quarter the New Testament met with no such rival as it confessedly met with in the Didache writings (*vide supra*). We shall discuss later the fact that Marcion was fortunate enough to find a form for the opposite undertaking in his *Antitheses,* and assigned to this work canonical authority.

[1] (As for me, my documents are Jesus Christ—the unquestionable documents, His Cross and His Death and Resurrection.) *Phil.*, 8.

with St Paul nor the others is there any demand for a new document. Why not? Just because they thought that they possessed it already in the Old Testament, in those prophetical passages to which they gave the widest compass. By introducing into the ancient Scriptures themselves the distinction, indeed the opposition, between the Law and the Gospel, by finding this distinction in all those passages which speak of something "new," of a new Covenant, of a First and a Second and the like, of an extension of the Covenant to the Gentiles, they felt that they already possessed the written document of the new message of salvation, the authority they required.[1]

But now a certain ambiguity, or at least an appearance of such, appears on the scene. Even St Paul is grievously affected by it. Where lies the boundary between Law and Prophets? Which is the Old and which is the New? Is it that everything in the Old Testament is new, and that there is only need of a right understanding to spy the "New" everywhere? Is thus the "Old" in the "Old Testament" merely a mischievous phantom that emanates from the stubborn unintelligence of the Jews?[2] Or is it that all in the Old Testament is indeed "New," but God has, for pedagogic reasons, veiled it with the appearance of the "Old"—in-

[1] See especially the Epistle of Barnabas, and Justin.

[2] This is the view of the author of the Epistle of Barnabas.

deed not only with the appearance, but with the "Old" itself, in accommodation with the character of the Jew; and that now, through Christ, all is unveiled for the Christian.[1] Or is a sharp distinction to be drawn between the moral and the ceremonial Law—the latter is abrogated, the former still in force? Or is the "New" a higher stage of development that does not deny its relationship to the "Old," but in a sense supplements it, or deepens the meaning and gives greater stringency to the demand, or lightens the yoke of the Old? Or, finally, are all these suppositions false? Is the "Old" absolutely and completely abolished because it was a grievous error ever to have regarded the Old Testament as the Word of God? There never was an "Old Covenant," and the Old Testament is thus unmasked: it is the work of Jews and, as such, is to be despised or even condemned.

Such were the difficulties which oppressed with ever-increasing weight the Christian in his controversy with the Jew and the Gnostic, and, above all, were a source of irritation to the life of the Churches and dominated the thought of their intellectual leaders (between A.D. 60 and 160). What way of deliverance from these perplexities was open? They needed an *authoritative document*, a *document* which, because it gave *a priori* the right standpoint, decided these questions once and for all. But

[1] This is the common view shared by Justin.

where was such a document to be found? The "correct" standpoint between Jew and Jewish Christian on the one hand and Marcion and Gnosticism on the other was given, in the firm determination of the important Churches to abide, with the original Apostles and St Paul, faithful to the Old Testament, and yet at the same time to appeal to written fundamental writings that testified to the transcendent claim of the New Covenant, and gave written authority to the "legisdatio in libertatem" in contrast to the "legisdatio in servitutem" of the same God.[1] No one that reads Justin's Dialogue with Typho but can receive the liveliest impression that the author is simply crying for a New Testament; but, seeing that he cannot produce it *directly as a fundamental document* he is compelled to write endless chapters and laboriously to construct it himself from the Old Testament and the history of Jesus (the Gospels)! If he could have quoted as the Word of God in strict sense *one only* of the dozens of appropriate passages in St Paul, and could have been able to refer to *books of the "New Covenant"*—how much simpler and shorter his whole task would have become!

(4) The fourth and last motive derives from the

[1] This meant the rejection of the views of "Barnabas" (an Old Covenant is a Jewish mistake), of Marcion and the Gnostics (the so-called Old Covenant together with the Old Testament is the work of another god), but also of the strict Jewish Christians (the "New Covenant" is essentially nothing new but is only the continuation and completion of the Old).

problem presented to the Church since the second century by the presence of a considerable Christian literature. A mass of Christian works had come into existence of extremely varied content (especially the Gnostic writings), some of which advanced high claims to authority and often afforded grievous scandal to simple believers. What is admissible, what is not admissible? What corresponds to Orthodoxy ("Orthognomy," Justin)? what contradicts it? What is "Catholic," and what not?—These were questions which became ever more burning, and necessitated an authoritative *selection* of what was trustworthy and good. And, besides, the more time advanced the more one was driven to distinguish between the "New" and the "Old"; for the Christian religion experienced what every religion—and every religious community—experiences—it began to worship its own past. *The more perplexing, troublous, and feeble its present appeared, the more precious and sacred became its own past, the time of creative energy, with all that belonged thereto.* Necessarily, therefore, the process of selection was governed, not only by the criterion "Catholic," but also by the criterion "Old," to which the more definite name "Apostolic" came to be attached. But what had been selected as orthodox and "Catholic" possessed as such a certain authority, which was still further enhanced if the additional predicate "Apostolic" ("old") could be attached to it.[1] The result of the working out of this fourth motive would therefore quite necessarily combine with what was demanded by the third motive: in the "Catholic" and "Apostolic" would be found fundamental, authoritative documents of the New Covenant.

We have now sketched the embryonic history of the New Testament in its leading motives.[2] This

[1] The task of selection was the more difficult in that, according to the earliest belief, he who speaks (or writes) of the Lord speaks under the influence of the Spirit of God (1 Cor. xii. 3; Didache iv. 1: ὅθεν ἡ κυριότης λαλεῖται ἐκεῖ κύριός ἐστιν. Old-fashioned Tertullian, *De Cultu*, i. 3: "Omnis scriptura ædificationi habilis divinitus inspirata est"). To select and reject was, therefore, a matter of serious responsibility. Seen from this point of view the New Testament is, therefore, a "remainder-product," and the belief in its inspiration is a mere relic of the much richer conception that the Spirit of Christ (of God) initiated and overruled every sincere word of testimony to Himself. The New Testament is thus a Remainder-product, and at the same time a new creation (as a collection of Apostolic-Catholic writings). In the former character it was determined by *rejection*, in the latter by *collection*.

[2] Motives which derived from the relations of the Churches with the surrounding heathen world can scarcely be included here. The apologists even after the creation of the New Testament found no need to change the old method of operating with the Old Testament alone, and only adding a little from the Gospel tradition. When dealing with heathen it was such an advantage to be able to appeal to scriptures of venerable antiquity that the new were left on one side; indeed Justin, one of the earliest apologists, makes more constant use of the new writings (the Gospels) and in controversy with the heathen thrusts them more conspicuously into the foreground, than any of his successors. The most important apologetic work of the primitive Church, Tertullian's *Apologeticum*, gives in reference to Christ only an historical sketch, which would necessarily have been understood by heathen to proceed from official "Acts of Pilate," while the Gospels are as good as ignored. Yet in making these remarks I do not wish to deny that in many particular cases of

history led to *written gospels* on the one hand, and on the other hand to the demand for a *fundamental document* of the New Covenant that would confute both Jewish Christian and Gnostic alike. Moreover, it led also to the demand that the orthodox (Catholic) writings should be separated from the mass of upstart, misleading works, and that at the same time special honour should be paid *to all that was "old"* (Apostolic). These needs and requirements would of themselves suggest the standard by which such books were chosen; but the task must have been easier in places where "Apostolic" articles of faith had become firmly established, and so a fixed standard for selection had been set up.[1] Thus an Old Testament with Christian interpretation or an enriched Old Testament no longer sufficed; for neither the one nor the other fulfilled

controversy of Christians with heathen it was not a great advantage to be able to appeal to a New Testament as well as to the Old Testament, and that complications must have occurred so long as this was not yet possible.

[1] Here is the point where the question of the connection between the growing New Testament and the Creed presents itself—the problem which Lessing was the first to state clearly. His solution is correct in the sense that the Catholic standard of orthodoxy, or Rule of Faith, is more ancient than the New Testament, and exercised an important influence on its compilation. The Muratorian Fragment in several passages affords a direct proof that this was so; but even without this testimony the fact would be proved. Lessing, however, has not shown, or at any rate has not sufficiently clearly shown, that every collection of sacred documents has an innate and unconquerable tendency to shake itself free from the conditions out of which it has arisen (*cf.* Second Part, § 1).

the needs that had grown up and now imperiously asserted themselves. In the motives which we have described the *New Testament exists in embryo.*

(*B*) But whence came the *authority* which was necessary for such a production ? Three points are here to be considered.

In the first place, in primitive Christendom, though every Christian was believed to have received the Spirit, certain members were regarded as being specially inspired, as being "bearers of the Spirit" κατ' ἐξοχήν. The directions of these "Apostles, Prophets, and Teachers" could not but be simply accepted and obeyed.[1] Though, on the one hand, their existence and activity might mean a hindrance to the formation of an authoritative written canon—for what need was there of Scriptures when one had living authorities ?—yet, on the other hand, they might act as promoters ; for if they gave any directions concerning written works, these also could not but be obeyed. In these "bearers of the Spirit" the Churches thus possessed, until far into the second century, authorities that could create what was *new* and could give to the new the seal of prescription. If in later days the bishop was asked what ought to be read in public,[2] there is no

[1] *Cf.* concerning these three, my *Missionsgeschichte,* 1², S. 267 ff., and my *Kirchenverfassung,* S. 18 ff. Their connection with Jewish tradition need not here be discussed.

[2] *Vide e.g.* Euseb., *H.E.*, vi. 12, 4, where Serapion, bishop of Antioch at the time of Septimius Severus, gives an important decision concerning the Gospel of Peter.

doubt that at earlier times the same question was addressed to the "Apostle" or the "Prophet" or the "Teacher," and that their authority sufficed.

In the second place, every circle of Christians that met together in the name of Jesus Christ and gave a direction or made a decision, felt and knew that it had the Holy Spirit or, in other words, the power of the Lord Jesus (1 Cor. v. 4) as leader and supporter. The formulæ: "The Holy Spirit and we have decided" (Acts xv. 28), or "What we have said, God has said through us" (1 Clem. ad Cor. 59), or "We have spoken or written through the Holy Spirit" (1 Clem. ad Cor. 63), were in constant use. But the Church in its solemn assembly was especially an organ of the Holy Spirit; and Sohm in his *Kirchenrecht* (vol. i.) is right in making this conception the source of the absolute powers of the "Synods," which indeed had developed from the Church assembly.[1] These powers extended also to the determination of what writings were to be accepted or rejected, publicly read or excluded. From this standpoint we can comprehend the peremptory expressions of the Muratorian Fragment ("recipi non potest"; "recipimus"; "legi oportet"; "se publicare in finem temporum non

[1] When in after times Constantine and his successors revered the œcumenical synods as instruments of the Holy Spirit, and Justinian treated the decisions of the first four Councils as equal to the four Gospels, a principle was at work which can be justified from the early history of the Church.

potest"; "nihil in totum recipimus"; ["rejicimus"]); or the similar statements of Tertullian: "non recipitur" (Apoc. Enoch); "a nobis quidem nihil omnino rejiciendum est quod pertineat ad nos";[1] "penes nos [istæ scripturæ] apocryphorum nomine damnantur";[2] "certi sumus nihil recipiendum quod non conspiret germanæ paraturæ";[3] "receptior apud ecclesias epistola Barnabæ"[4] —they are intended to be taken as decisions of the Churches. That, moreover, the judgment of the Churches concerning the admissibility of books to the sacred canon depended in some cases at least upon direct synodical decisions, is baldly stated by Tertullian (*De Pudic.*, 10): "Sed cederem tibi, si scriptura Pastoris non *ab omni concilio ecclesiarum*, etiam vestrarum, inter apocrypha et falsa indicaretur."[5] The Community, therefore, in solemn assembly, and under the guidance of the Holy Spirit, was felt to have the power to accept or not to accept into the Canon, and *this power was also consciously exercised.*[6]

[1] *De Cultu*, i. 3.
[2] *De Anima*, 2.
[3] *Loc. cit.*
[4] *De Pudic.*, 20.

[5] Also in *De Baptism*, 17, it is evidently the intention of Tertullian to bring about a decree of the Church which would annul the too hasty reception of the *Acta Pauli* as a genuine document.

[6] Augustine speaks quite frankly (*c. Faustum*, xxii. 79) of "sancti et docti homines," as compilers of the New Testament ("Legunt scripturas apocryphas Manichæi, a nescio quibus sutoribus fabularum sub apostolorum nomine scriptas, quæ suorum scriptorum temporibus *in auctoritatem sanctæ ecclesiæ recipi mererentur, si sancti et docti homines, qui tunc in hac vita erant et examinare talia poterant, eos*

Thirdly and lastly, there is another circumstance that must not be overlooked. The greater became the distance in time from the Apostolical Age the more sacred became the series of writings that had Catholic character and Apostolic title, *just because of these properties and the distance.* They thus acquired such inward and outward authority that the Churches could not bring themselves to believe that they had the power either to accept or to reject them.[1] We have already touched upon the concept

vera locutores esse cognoscerent"). A valuable piece of information (*cf.* Origen, *Præf. in Luc.*)! The legends that the Apostles themselves, or the Apostle John, compiled the New Testament first appear in the Middle Ages, and are worthless. It is, therefore, surprising that Overbeck has no scruple in appealing to this very late legend to support his hypothesis concerning the predominant influence of "John" (*i.e.* of the Fourth Gospel) in the formation of the Canon of the Gospels (*Das Johannesev.*, 1911, S. 486, "In ancient legends (!) in which John appears as the founder of the Canon of the Gospels, indeed sometimes of the whole Canon of the New Testament, one may well recognise an echo of the original course of events if this went as I suppose." S. 490: "There is in existence an ecclesiastical legend that the Apostle John was the founder of the Canon of the Gospels, indeed of the Canon generally. This legend, late though it is, and in content on the whole unacceptable, may, nevertheless, quite justly be appealed to as a confused historical reminiscence of an actual occurrence of Christian antiquity such as I have sketched.") With what scorn would Overbeck have overwhelmed a critic that had dared to take a similar legend so seriously!

[1] We may imagine the process as follows: From the first ages, the ages of enthusiasm onwards, every Christian writing counted as "inspired" (*vide supra*). In course of time, as the number of Christian writings increased and their contents became ever more varied, this estimate of value, this feeling of reverence, became weaker and more vague. But now a new valuation according to the standard of the Apostolic-Catholic gradually won its way in the

" Catholic " ; in the next paragraphs we shall deal in more detail with the concept " Apostolic." Here we need only state the fact that the importance which everything " Apostolic-Catholic," either in content or in title, had acquired during the second century because of the Gnostic controversy was so great that in face of it the Churches felt that they had lost all right to decision and could only adopt a purely passive attitude. The decision is decision no longer, but mere *acquiescence*; they accept with all the consequences. Even in the case of Acta Pauli in Carthage, which Tertullian mentions, it cannot have been otherwise. When this book, which claimed to bring from the Apostolic Age a description of the history and teaching of St Paul, reached Carthage, it was *as a matter of course* accepted as having authority for the Church, and this practically meant that it was attached to the second collection of sacred writings that at that time already existed. One could only succeed in removing it from the Canon if one could unmask it and prove that it was a late and therefore a misleading work, and this is what Tertullian does. Naturally all would have been over with the book

Church. But Apostolic-Catholic did not mean less divine. This change is only one symptom of the grand historical revolution from enthusiasm to ecclesiasticism, from the spirit to the letter combined with the spirit. Like prophecy in earlier days, all that was Catholic and Apostolic had to be accepted as authoritative, and no one could criticise it.

if it could have been convicted of heresy, but in this case that was not so easy.

To sum up: At first, in the period when foundations were being laid, men were living who had the power to determine books as authoritative and who made use of their power as the need for such books arose. Then came a moment after which the collection of sacred books could only, so to speak, itself create or, rather, extend itself—namely, the moment when the conviction arose that every work that was Apostolic and Catholic belonged to an authoritative group. Other authorities could now have scarcely any voice in the matter, for once the Apostolic-Catholic character of a work was established the only right left to Christians was that of acquiescence. Nevertheless, in practice, this principle by no means established itself quite securely and absolutely. In the first place, the concept "Apostolic" was by no means clear. Did it imply the Twelve Apostles alone? or the Twelve and other Apostolic persons? or the Apostolic Age generally? And, secondly, as we shall see immediately, another and an incommensurable factor was involved, namely, the factor of *Custom*.

(*C*) The third question which we have yet to consider is the question—Supposing the necessity in idea of the New Testament, how did it come into actual existence? Motives by themselves do not create, and even if authority is at hand with power to realise motives, still there is always need of practical conditions in order to give life and form to what is possible and desirable. Such practical conditions were, however, present. In the first place, there existed a body of writings that was more or less fitted to satisfy the requirements—the Gospels at the earlier date, and in the following period every work that was old (Apostolic) and Catholic as well. But this was not enough to make them formally Scriptures of a Second Covenant. Justin, indeed, with a certain Christian assurance, speaks not only of "our doctrines," but also of "our writings" (*Apol.*, i. 28) side by side with the Old Testament, but as yet he knows nothing of Scriptures of the "New Covenant."

But he knew—and this is the second point—of a practice, in use in the Churches, of reading aloud in public worship the "memorabilia of the Apostles" (the Gospels) *or* the "writings of the prophets."[1] Here we light upon the fact that was of supreme importance for the realisation of the idea of the New Testament. Above all, *it was because Christian writings were in public worship actually treated like the Old Testament,*[2] *without being simply included in the body of the old Canon, that the idea of a second sacred collection could be realised.*[3] This was the

[1] *Apol.*, i. 67.

[2] Note the "or."

[3] Behind this public reading lay not only the historical motive but also the motive of moral and religious edification, as is proved

case in the first place with the Gospels. In actual practice these writings gradually came to be treated in the same way as the Old Testament, and so for half a century they stood side by side with the ancient Scriptures, and very soon with a dignity practically equal to that of the Old Testament. But we have sure evidence that other writings were likewise read at public worship, though perhaps not at first as a regular practice; for Dionysius, Bishop of Corinth (about A.D. 170), tells us that the Corinthian Christians still continued to read in public worship the epistle written by Clement from the Roman Church about A.D. 95, and that they would likewise read the new letter which they had just received from Rome.[1] If this happened in the case of important letters between Churches, what doubt can there be that it was so also above all with the epistles of St Paul—so unique, so incomparable—in Corinth and Rome, in Philippi and Thessalonica, in Ephesus, Hierapolis, and Colossæ, and not only in these places but wherever collections of Pauline epistles had arrived.[2] They would cer-

by the sermon that regularly followed the lection, and, moreover, by the practice of private reading. Concerning the latter practice, see my book, *Bible Reading in the Early Church* (Williams & Norgate). Thus practical piety also had its share in the creation of the New Testament.

[1] Euseb., *H.E.*, iv. 23, 11.

[2] Much intensive study has been devoted to the problem presented by the compilation of the thirteen (fourteen) Pauline epistles, with but meagre results. It is no longer possible to discover where the great final collection took place. From 1 Clement we may be sure

tainly be read publicly though not with the same regularity as the Gospels, and not as an alternative to the Scriptures of the Old Testament. The Johannine Apocalypse too, in its present form, dating from the last days of Domitian, was edited for reading in the Church (i. 3) and naturally not for a single reading only, which would have been quite profitless.[1] And though what was read is not indeed yet ἡ γραφή, still it could not but gradually come very near to the γραφή in the estimation of hearers who heard it again and again read aloud side by side with the Old Testament.[2] This explains how it happens that before the rise of the New Testament isolated instances occur in which

that a collection of several epistles then existed in Rome, and was treated, so to speak, as public property of the Church. Twenty to thirty years later the collection was certainly in existence in several Churches far distant from one another. This is enough for our purpose.

[1] Compare also the directions that Hermas gives in reference to the public reading of his book (*Vis.*, ii. 4).

[2] The inner relationship of "written Word" with "lection" comes out strikingly in the prologue (by Tertullian) to the *Passio Perpetuæ*, which will occupy us again later. Here we read: "Si vetera fidei exempla, et dei gratiam testificantia et ædificationem hominis operantia, *propterea in litteris sunt digesta, ut lectione eorum* . . . et deus honoretur et homo confortetur, cur non et *nova documenta* æque utrique causæ convenientia et *digerantur?* . . . Itaque et nos . . . prophetias et visiones novas . . . ad instrumentum ecclesiæ deputatas . . . necessario et *digerimus* et ad gloriam dei *lectione* celebramus." Yet it ought not to be overlooked that when Tertullian wrote these words the terms "the written Word" and "lectio" had already probably a more exclusive relationship than they had sixty or even thirty years earlier. The farther back one goes the freer was the choice of what was read at public service.

the Gospel is quoted with γέγραπται,[1] or in which a passage from a Pauline Epistle is adduced, together with passages from the Old Testament, as a quotation from Scripture.[2] On the other hand, it ought not to be overlooked that, through this practice of public lection, *usages* would necessarily be formed in the separate Churches which, in that they affected the development of the future New Testament, created differences that had necessarily to be overcome if any unity was to be attained. So far as the "lectio" allowed *usages* to arise side by side with the reading of the Old Testament, it unconsciously prepared the way for a second sacred collection, but it could neither dot the "i" nor lead to unity.

Public Lection was unquestionably a particularly strong agent in establishing the second sacred collection *however little it was qualified to create inward unity of choice and to determine the limits of a Canon.* But when one has mentioned public lection one must also remember another factor,

[1] (It is written.)

[2] For the former, see Barn. iv. 14, and, later, 2 Clement ii. 4; xiii. 4; for the latter Polyc. xii. 1 (only preserved in the somewhat untrustworthy Latin version). The passage 2 Peter iii. 16 would be very important for the equation Pauline Epistles = Holy Scripture if the date of this late epistle could be more definitely determined. This transference of the authority of ἡ γραφή to isolated passages of evangelic writings (before there was as yet a New Testament) has its parallel in the quotations, with the formulæ λέγει or γέγραπται, from Jewish or Christian apocalypses, that did not form part of the Canon. See Ephes. v. 14; 1 Clem. xxiii.; 2 Clem. xi., etc.

quite remote and different in character, that most probably played a part here. It is well known that the reformer Marcion (scarcely later than A.D. 140), who rejected the Old Testament, gave to his Church a collection of sacred writings consisting of a critical edition of the Lucan Gospel and ten Pauline Epistles (likewise critically edited); and that he assigned to this collection the same authority that the Old Testament possessed among the Jews and the Christians of the greater Churches.[1] It is also well known that about the same time Gnostic sects, which likewise rejected the Old Testament, appealed to *Gospels and Pauline Epistles* as an authentic *instrumentum doctrinæ*.[2] The idea and the realisation of a *new*, sacred, specifically Christian collection of writings, in addition to the Gospels, appears first among the Marcionites and

[1] It is interesting that Marcion also added to his collection a work of his own as a canonical book—a work which he called *Antitheses*, showing the *discordance* between the Old Testament and the Gospel. That which nearly happened yet did not happen in the Church (*vide supra*), namely, the construction of a *canonical* book showing the *concordance* between the Old Testament and the Gospel history, happened with Marcion *in the contrary sense*, and his book seemed to him so important that he formally canonised it for his Church. Unfortunately we can form no clear impression of the form of this work because we only possess fragments of it. Catholic Christians must have regarded it as a regular work of the Devil. And indeed, from their point of view, a more evil and dangerous book could not have been imagined.

[2] See the letter of Ptolemy to Flora which may well be taken in evidence for Valentinus himself, and other pieces of testimony as to the Valentinians, Basilideans, etc. Still, "the Lord" is always properly given the first place.

the Gnostics—and quite naturally; for, seeing that they rejected the Old Testament, they were compelled to set up another *litera scripta* in its place. *That which could only arise in the Church as the result of a complicated process of development, because at first the Old Testament was a formidable obstacle, this naturally and necessarily makes its appearance in the heretical sects, because without some such second sacred collection they would have possessed absolutely no instrumentum doctrinæ.* Can we think that this step had any influence upon the great Churches? They could hardly have allowed themselves to be consciously influenced; but in history conscious influences are by no means the only influences, nor are they the strongest.[1] The simple and notorious

[1] From this point of view we must doubtless admit that the motive of compulsion had a place in the creation of the New Testament. The Church was in a sense forced to take this step, and the step was not altogether to her advantage. We see this indeed quite clearly in Tertullian's treatise, *De Præscript. Heret.* The existence of the New Testament in itself and as a collection of equally authoritative books presented great difficulties to him in his polemic; for how could one prevent false interpretations, and how much there was in these writings that, taken literally, was actually questionable and had now to be justified by laborious interpretation (so with Irenæus, but the embarrassment is specially noticeable in Tertullian). The rather idle question whether apart from the conflict with heresy a New Testament would ever have come into existence is to be answered in the affirmative, for, as has been already suggested by our previous discussion, the idea of the New Covenant and the tendency to establish and confirm the idea would necessarily have resulted in calling the second sacred collection into being. This, however, does not prevent us from recognising that the New Testament as it stands and the history of its development bear traces of the element of *compulsion*. As an Apostolic-Catholic compilation

fact that a new sacred collection was in existence among those heretics must have worked upon the Church as effectually as the composition of the Lutherian Catechism and of the articles and other professions of faith of the Reformers influenced the Roman Catholic Church in the sixteenth century.[1] In the next sections we shall go more

it was constructed as a means of defence rather than of attack. If the point of view of the compilation had not been anti-Gnostic and Apostolic-Catholic the Acts of the Apostles would hardly have been included, the Johannine Apocalypse would almost certainly have been excluded, and the Pauline Epistles would have stood as a sort of appendix.

[1] See my *Lehrbuch der Dogmengeschichte*, I^4, S. 380 f.: "The Church in excluding certain persons on the ground of apostolic rules of whatever kind, and in relation to the Old Testament, would not appear in a satisfactory position either in her own eyes or in the eyes of her opponents so long as she herself recognised that apostolic writings were in existence, and so long as these heretics appealed to apostolic writings. She was compelled to claim for herself everything that had a right to the name 'Apostolic,' to take it out of the hands of the heretics, and to show that with her it exists as authentic and stands in the highest esteem. Hitherto she had remained satisfied with proving her title from the Old Testament, and thus tracing herself, far past her real origin, back to the beginning of all things. Marcion, however, and the Gnostics first pointed out with tremendous emphasis that Christianity had its origin in Christ; that all that is Christian must actually satisfy the test of the (genuine) Apostolic teaching; that the assumed identity of Christian common sense with Apostolic Christianity did not exist; indeed (in the case of Marcion), that the Apostles themselves contradicted one another. By the last objection the Church was compelled to accept the field of battle chosen by her opponents. But the task of proving this contested identity was insoluble because every point upon which an argument could be based was a matter of controversy. 'Unconscious logic,' *i.e.* the logic of self-preservation, could point out one only way: the Church must collect everything that was Apostolic, declare herself to be its sole and rightful owner, and weld together the Apostolic

closely into the question of Marcion's Bible; for its inner arrangement and its division into Gospel and Apostles in their significance for the formation of the New Testament of the Church must be considered, and, as we shall see, our conjecture that here also influence has come into play will be confirmed. But stronger than this positive influence must have been the influence of the *antagonism* to which the Church was aroused by Marcionism. This also would suggest the idea of Apostolic-Catholic. All such writings must be collected and compiled in opposition to what was false and spurious.

The fact that most valuable, important, and primitive Christian writings were at hand, further, the practice of public reading, and, lastly, the examples of the Marcionites and Gnostics, which must have provoked both imitation and opposition, explain how the motives, which suggested the origin of the Church's New Testament, could realise themselves, and how the authorities that could create it came into action. But we must still take another fact into consideration before we can understand how the collection of works came to be the "Canon of the New Covenant."

A simple "collection" of writings need not be final; rather it can even more or less purposely be

so closely with the Canon of the Old Testament that for the future right interpretation was secured." Further, she would be compelled to set up a rule of faith as a rule for interpretation, and finally to assign to herself the sole right of interpretation.

left open, especially if it serves ends (such as public reading) which do not forbid enrichment from the stores of the present. And yet a collection of fundamental documents has already *the tendency to become final,* and certainly a collection of fundamental documents of a *Covenant* carries in itself the idea of complete finality. It is also certain that a compilation of writings is always in danger of disintegration if it is not in some way limited, in *idea* at least. A hundred years ago Novalis advanced the very reasonable question : "Who declared the Bible (the Canon of the New Testament) to be closed ?" Our answer to the question is : The idea, firmly held, that the new books were fundamental documents *of the Second Covenant* which God had established through Jesus Christ, was the intellectual originator of the "closed" *instrumentum novum.* When, then, did the idea of the New Covenant come to be firmly grasped ? Now no one could have had a more strongly practical and historical hold upon it than the Apostle Paul (*vide supra*) ; yet he never thought of "books" of the Covenant, nor was he in a position to distinguish a classical Covenant-time from the time that came afterwards. Gradually, however, new "books" appeared, as we have seen, and gradually with the advance of time the idea ever more strongly insinuated itself that the Apostolic Age, with all that belonged to it, was classical ; it set up an authoritative model of perfection to which subsequent ages could no longer attain.

Then the Montanist movement made its appearance and, with all the force of primitive energy, struggled against the Christian mediocrity that veiled itself in this assumed humility. Far from allowing that the highest lay in the past and was now only inherited as an "objective" legacy, the Montanists proclaimed that the highest both in revelation and in doctrine had now first arrived in the Paraclete, and that no final covenant of unapproachable sanctity had been given in the Apostolic Age, but that continually and increasingly the *Novum* and *Novissimum* reveals itself in prophecy, vision, and admonition.[1] It was in opposition to this position that the leaders of the Church first thought out and developed the idea of a covenant established and finally sealed in the manifestation of Christ and in the work of His Apostles, so that they were able to consistently reject *every* work which did not belong to this primitive epoch. *By this procedure the Testamentum Novum (as a collection of the books of the New Covenant) was really first firmly established and forthwith finally limited in conception at least.* The era of

[1] It is scarcely necessary to say that Montanism with the claims that it advanced could never have arisen if a New Testament had been already in existence. (The same is true of the appearance of the so-called Alogi, who are still, according to my belief, to be placed in Asia Minor.)

enthusiasm was closed, and, so far as the present time was concerned, the Spirit—using Tertullian's words (*Adv. Prax.*, 1)—was actually chased away—chased into a book! [1] Naturally it was a long, long time before all was brought to a firm conclusion—there were too many "usages" and other variations still to be overcome—but since the end of the Montanist controversy, and entirely as a result of that controversy, the collection of the books of the

[1] The New Testament opens and legitimises the period of the Christendom of the second order or the period of legitimised Christianity. Prophets, to say nothing of Apostles, are now no longer possible, *Ἑκαστος ἔχει χαρισμα ἀπὸ θεοῦ, ὁ μὲν οὕτως, ὁ δὲ οὕτως, οἱ ἀπόστολοι δὲ ἐν πᾶσι πεπληρωμένοι* (Clem. Alex., *Strom.*, iv. 21, 135). But again still more emphatically Tertullian—the same man who when he remembers his Montanism speaks so differently—writes (*De Exhort.*, 4): "Spiritum quidem dei etiam fideles habent, sed non omnes fideles apostoli . . . proprie enim apostoli spiritum sanctum habent, qui plene habent in operibus prophetiæ . . . non ex parte, quod ceteri." Thus the Apostles have the Spirit *proprie et plene* like the Lord! What real Christian could dare to compare himself with them, and how could a prophet possibly arise among those who thought thus! The New Testament, though not with one stroke, brought to an end the condition of things in which a chance Christian inspired by the Spirit could claim to give authoritative decisions and directions and could enrich with his fancy the history of the past and foretell the events of the future so as to command the faith of his hearers. Moreover, through the New Testament, it came to be recognised that the Christianity of the post-Apostolic epoch was only *secondary* and *particular* and, therefore, could never be authoritative nor serve as a standard. In refutation of an epistle of the Montanist Themison, who was also a Confessor—an epistle that was evidently addressed as a manifesto to the whole Church—the anti-Montanist, Apollonius, writes (Euseb., *H.E.*, v. 18, 5); *ἐτόλμησεν, μιμούμενος τὸν ἀπόστολον, καθολικήν τινα συνταξάμενος ἐπιστολήν, κατηχεῖν τοὺς ἄμεινον αὐτοῦ πεπιστευκότας.* More will be said on this point in the second part.

New Covenant stands complete in idea. In this connection it is therefore not by accident that we first find the expression "the books of the Old Covenant"[1] used by Melito, Bishop of Sardis, about A.D. 170–180, *a native of Asia Minor* and an opponent of the Montanists. We may with the greatest probability conclude that one who used this expression already recognised a collection of works as books of the New Covenant. What books these were cannot be ascertained so long as we must bewail the loss of the works of Melito, yet this is not a matter of the first importance. The one fact of decisive importance is that he does actually know books under such a title. And Melito, with his knowledge of "Books of the New Testament," does not stand alone in Asia Minor. The anonymous anti-Montanist of Euseb., *H.E.*, v. 16, 3 (about A.D. 192–193) writes: δεδιὼς καὶ ἐξευλαβούμενος μή πῃ δόξω τισὶν ἐπισυνγράφειν ἢ ἐπιδιατάσσεσθαι τῷ τῆς τοῦ εὐαγγελίου καινῆς διαθήκης λόγῳ, ᾧ μήτε προσθεῖναι μήτε ἀφελεῖν δυνατὸν τῷ κατὰ τὸ εὐαγγέλιον αὐτὸ πολιτεύεσθαι προῃρημένῳ.[2] The fear that the publishing of a *written work* might awaken the suspicion that one wished to add something to the doctrine of the New Covenant as given in the Gospel

[1] Euseb., *H.E.*, iv. 26, 14.

[2] (In fear and dread, lest in writing I might seem to be adding to the injunctions of the Word of the New Covenant of the Gospel, to add to or to subtract from which is unthinkable for one who chooses to live in accordance with the Gospel itself.)

could not have arisen unless *writings* of the New Covenant, *and these not only Gospels*, were already in existence. Of equal importance is the evidence afforded by Tertullian. This writer, who as a Catholic churchman and opponent of heresy and as a Montanist is always in conflict with himself, on the one hand, when he, writing in cool blood, uses the expression *Novum Testamentum* or *libri Novi Testamenti*, on the other hand, in all the excitement of controversy he denounces in his prologue to the *Passio Perpetuæ* those Churchmen who proclaim a New Testament finally closed, and would therefore grant no place in it, or side by side with it, to the contemporary utterances of the *novissima prophetia*. All goes to show that, though the Gnostic crisis did indeed create the idea of Apostolic-Catholic as applied to writings, and brought about a *selection* of works which included the whole material of the future New Testament, *it was the Montanist, not the Gnostic crisis, that brought the idea of the New Testament to final realisation and created the conception of a closed Canon.* The Muratorian Fragment sets the seal as it were to the decision of the Church never to admit a later (non-Apostolic) writing into the New Testament, when it declares that "the Shepherd" of Hermas, who wrote "nuperrime temporibus nostris," ought not "in finem temporum" to be received into the sacred Canon, and by the almost insulting severity of its rejection of Montanus: "Una cum Basilide (!) Asianum Cataphrygum constitutorem [rejicimus]."[1] Although the author of the Fragment expressly leaves the Canon of Apostolic writings still open—for him only the writings of the Old Testament prophets form a "completus numerus" (line 79), not the writings of the "Apostles"—yet in fact he so good as closes it completely; for, according to his theory, acceptance could be granted only to those Apostolic writings that hitherto had been accidentally overlooked.

Thus the second Canon came to take its place beside the first. The first was preserved because the God of Salvation was felt to be also the God of Creation, and because Christians following St Paul held fast to the historical conception that the Covenant given in Jesus Christ was preceded not only by prophecies but also by a *Covenant*, naturally imperfect because suited to the childhood of mankind. This conception has an artificial touch of which it can only be relieved if one gives it the universal form of the "Education of mankind" and strips it of particularistic traits; and it would probably not have held its ground, and the Old Testament would have perished in the Church as it did among the Gnostics, if the book had not been

[1] Montanus could be ranked with Basilides, because among the adherents of the latter two prophets, Barkoph and Barkabbas, stood in the highest honour.

so indispensable for Apologetics. So long as the truth of religions was measured by their age the apologist simply could not do without the Old Testament. With it he could prove that Christianity went back to the creation of mankind. How could he forgo so great an advantage that was only to be gained through the preservation and recognition of the Old Testament!

Naturally the Old Testament could only continue in force under the condition that, while its essential equality with the new Canon, as shown in prophecy and through the employment of allegorical interpretation, was recognised, yet from a second point of view it was regarded as *inferior.* This is at once clear from the works of Irenæus the first ecclesiastical author that operates with the two Canons. The Old Testament as "legisdatio in servitutem" has become inferior since the appearance of Christ. The books of the "legisdatio in libertatem" outshine it and throw it into the background. And though Irenæus does not yet know of a *closed* second Canon and though he does not assign to it the name "the books of the New Covenant," still in his exposition he proceeds as if it were already closed—the name only is wanting, the thing itself is practically in existence for him. The books of the new collection are on the one hand the documents of the New Covenant and on the other hand the Apostolic-Catholic books of the Church.[1] Because they are the latter they are also the former and *vice versa.* With these lofty predicates the New Testament was given in the sense in which it has remained in force unto the present day.[2]

[1] Of the Church—ἐκκλησιαστικαὶ γραφαί: this term now also makes its appearance. During the conflict with the Gnostics and Montanists, and because of the conflict, the Church had come to recognise that she belonged both to heaven and to earth. Before this she knew herself only as something heavenly, high, and exalted, now she feels that she belongs also to earth. The affinity between herself and the new Canon finds at once strong expression in the Muratorian Fragment: the New Testament is the *book of the Church* in opposition to heathen, heretics—*and enthusiasts*; the seven epistles of the Apocalypse and the epistles of St Paul to seven churches are in truth addressed to the *one Church* spread over all the world (lines 47–59); the epistles to Philemon, Titus, and Timothy are "in honore ecclesiæ"; for "in ordinatione *ecclesiasticæ* disciplinæ sanctificatæ sunt" (lines 59–63). Nothing false can be received "*into the Catholic Church*" (lines 63–68). The Epistle of Jude and the two epistles of John "*in catholica habentur*" (lines 68 f.). The Wisdom of Solomon was written "*in honorem catholicæ*" (so we must construe lines 69–71). The Apocalypse of Peter, "according to the view of some of our people," ought not to be read "*in ecclesia*" (lines 71–73). The Shepherd of Hermas should not be read aloud before the people "*in ecclesia*" (lines 73 ff.). The new collection belongs to the *Church* as an *earthly* as well as a heavenly entity, serves the ends of the *Church,* and becomes her book in the same sense (*vide* especially Origen) that the Old Testament was and is the book of the Jewish Theocracy.

[2] Its text now at last (*i.e.* in the third century) became stable because the *letter* now had become most important. In the second century there was a fair amount of correction of the text of the Gospels even in orthodox communities. But seeing that the corrections were mostly due to conformation with the text of the other Gospels and doctrinal corrections were most infrequent, we have no right to conclude that the texts were still regarded as absolutely free for correction. Already at the time of Justin such a one as he would have certainly shrunk from laying a hand upon the Memorabilia of

§ 2. *Why is it that the New Testament also contains other books beside the Gospels, and appears as a compilation with two divisions* ("*Evangelium*" *and* "*Apostolus*") *?*

In the foregoing section hints have been given which prepare for the answering of this question; but the problem has not yet been set in clear light. How great it is must be realised by everyone who reflects only for a moment. In the New Testament letters which serve momentary and particular needs are set on a level of equal value with the Gospels; what is merely personal with what is of

the Apostles, and Dionysius of Corinth complains only of the arbitrary correction made by heretics (Euseb., *H.E.*, iv. 23, 12: ἐπιστολὰς ἀδελφῶν ἀξιωσάντων με γράφαι ἔγραψα, καὶ ταύτας οἱ τοῦ διαβόλου ἀπόστολοι ζιξανίων γεγέμικαν, ἃ μὲν ἐξαιροῦντες, ἃ δὲ προστιθέντες· οἷς τὸ οὐαὶ κεῖται. οὐ θαυμαστὸν ἄρα εἰ καὶ τῶν κυριακῶν ῥαδιουργῆσαί τινες ἐπιβέβληνται γραφῶν, ὁπότε καὶ ταῖς οὐ τοιαύταις ἐπιβεβουλεύκασιν. Conformation, however, did not count as correction. The transmission of the text of the Pauline Epistles is excellent. It is, moreover, interesting to see how long the Gospels, in spite of the creation of the New Testament, still kept in the foreground and occupied a certain separate position. Even at the beginning of the fourth century Alexander of Alexandria (Theodoret, *H.E.*, i. 4) calls God the giver of the Law, the prophets, *and the Gospels*. This special distinction of the Gospels never quite ceased in the practice of the Church in public worship, especially in the East, and in connection with private reading. The enormous number of manuscripts of the Gospels, when compared with the manuscripts of the Apostolus, of itself proves this. Among Protestants this distinction between the two parts of the Canon has become more faintly marked than among the Catholic Churches; in this Protestantism has about it a touch of Marcionitism. Yet also of the Catholic Churches it is true that in hermeneutics and dogmatics "The Lord" is subsumed under "the Apostolic." It is partly otherwise only in Monasticism and in the theory of neo-Protestantism.

universal import; the Apostles with Christ; their work with His work! In a compilation which is invested with Divine authority we must read: "Drink a little wine for thy stomach's sake," and "my cloak I left at Troas." Side by side with the words of Divine mercy and loving-kindness in the Gospels we meet with outbreaks of passionate personal strife in the Epistles; side by side with the stories of the Passion and Resurrection, the dry notes of the diary of a missionary journey!

He who would show how two absolutely disparate entities have yet come together can only solve the problem if he can prove that they form the extreme wings of a complex whole that is governed by an idea. The idea in question here is the idea of *Tradition*. One of the great problems which has silently dominated the inner history of the Church for centuries is the problem, "*Scripture and Tradition*." *In the compilation of the New Testament this problem already, to a certain extent, found a solution; indeed, properly speaking, the strivings and conflicts that have taken place since this solution,* i.e. *since the creation of the New Testament, are all of them only of secondary import. The main battle was long since fought and decided in favour of Tradition when the New Testament was compiled and in the very fact of its compilation;* but, unfortunately, historians have not yet generally recognised this truth. The New Testament itself, when compared with what

Jesus purposed, said, and was, is already a tradition which overlies and obscures. When then we speak to-day of the antagonism and conflict between Scripture and Tradition, the tradition in question is a *second* tradition.

The compilation of the New Testament out of the "Gospels," with their Apostolic titles and the "Apostolus," is clearly the expression of two convictions: (*A*) that in a certain sense the Apostles are equal to Christ in that they, being chosen not only to be His witnesses, but also dispensers of His power, are His continuation; and (*B*) that the *attestation* of a revelation is not less important than its *content.* When did these convictions make their appearance? How and under what circumstances did they attach themselves to books? How was it that under their influence the Acts of the Apostles came to be accepted into the Canon, and that such strong preference was given to St Paul?

(*A*) Sceptical critics of the Synoptic Gospels have thought it necessary to disintegrate with special stringency the tradition concerning the relationship between our Lord and His twelve Disciples.[1] Indeed

[1] According to the delusive canon, which, unfortunately, so many scholars of to-day follow in the criticism of the Gospels, that passages which *can also* have sprung from developments of the Apostolic and later ages *must* therefore have so sprung. For example: Jesus speaks of future persecutions; such persecutions actually occurred; hence these sayings have been constructed *ex eventu* and do not belong to Him. Albert Schweitzer does well to protest strongly against such a method.

even the number twelve, and with it every special reference to "chosen" disciples, is objected to. In my opinion, criticism is here running on false lines. Sayings like: Ἐγὼ διατίθεμαι ὑμῖν, καθὼς διέθετό μοι ὁ πατήρ μου βασιλείαν, ἵνα ἔσθητε καὶ πίνητε ἐπὶ τῆς τραπέζης μου ἐν τῇ βασιλείᾳ μου, καὶ καθῆσθε ἐπὶ θρόνων τὰς δώδεκα φυλὰς κρίνοντες τοῦ Ἰσραήλ (St Luke xxii. 29 f.);[1] or Ὁ δεχόμενος ὑμας ἐμὲ δέχεται, καὶ ὁ ἐμὲ δεχόμενος δέχεται τὸν ἀποστείλαντά με (St Matt. x. 40), the fundamental thought of which is found both in St Mark and in *Q*, cannot but be accepted as essentially trustworthy.

There also appears to be no special reason to doubt that Jesus during His lifetime sent out twelve disciples on a mission in Palestine and that they actually undertook this mission and returned to Him again. All in all, sayings of Jesus must have existed that referred to the disciples as sent out on the mission, and that offered them the prospect of the highest authority and of even Messianic powers when the "Kingdom" was established. On this supposition alone can we explain the authority of the Twelve in the Church.

For the Twelve, after our Lord had departed from them and was glorified, played in reality an insignificant *rôle*. This is only intelligible on the assumption that an express command of Jesus to begin a mission in grand style after His death did

[1] Notice the Jewish horizon of this saying.

not exist. As a matter of fact the Twelve remained in Jerusalem and, apart from awaiting the time when they would take up their office in the coming Kingdom, the building up of the Church in Jerusalem, of which task they were moreover soon relieved by James the Lord's brother, remained the sole object of their existence. We have no certain knowledge that any one of them, except St Peter and St John, ever went on mission ; but there is no doubt that their authority as the Twelve remained firmly established, because they were regarded as the confidants of Jesus and as the future *judges* at the establishment of the Messianic Kingdom.[1]

The recognition of the lofty status of the Twelve, an authority that was at first naturally bound up with that of the Mother Church in Jerusalem, went forth with St Paul and the other missionaries into the Gentile world. These spoke of the Twelve Apostles as of authorities for all that they in

[1] It is not here our business to investigate whether the commission to the Twelve to forgive sins, to " bind and loose," is to be traced back to Jesus Himself, or whether the story was first conceived at a later date. But it is certain that, just as the unhistoric command to go forth into all the world (Matt. xxviii. 19) belongs to the tradition that had taken form in *Palestine*, so also the conception of the Apostles as being dispensers of forgiving power or of the "Spirit" has the same place of origin. The sacramental power assigned to the Twelve, and their " knowledge of the mysteries of the Kingdom of Heaven," whencesoever these ideas derived, were certainly of highest importance for the supreme veneration in which they were held by the Gentile Churches, who set the Twelve so near to the Lord and at last united them with Him in the New Testament. There is, however, no doubt that these ideas proceeded from Palestine.

common brought with them from the motherland of the new movement, and also in part for that which they themselves built on that foundation. And so now appeared that strange phenomenon —the "Twelve Apostles" as the court of highest instance and of fundamental authority. Soon also the belief took shape that Christ had committed the continuation and expansion of His work to the Twelve once for all, and so completely, that every real mission is subordinate to them and receives from them its content and authority.[1] The Roman Church writes about A.D. 95: "The Apostles were made evangelists to us by the Lord Christ (mark well: 'the Apostles,' not Peter and Paul); Jesus the Christ was sent by God. Thus Christ is from God and the Apostles from Christ. He and they came into being in harmony from the will of God."[2] Since the end of the first century the Apostles already seemed to the Gentile Church like a multiplication of the Christ.[3] The Church is built upon them as a foundation: in the New Jerusalem the

[1] Indeed at an early date the general conception was that the mission to the world had been actually completed by the Apostles—for the end was near and before it could come the Gospel must have been preached everywhere—and that present missions were only an aftergleaning.

[2] 1 Clem. 42.

[3] This conception must have been the more acceptable to Gentile Christians seeing that Christ Himself had not come to them. Legends of missions undertaken by Apostles soon came to be invented; none dared to invent one for Christ (yet one must remember the Abgar legend).

twelve foundation stones of the city wall bear the names of the twelve Apostles of the Lamb.[1] If one spoke of the commands of Christ, one added the Apostles.[2] What Serapion says at the beginning of the third century (Euseb., *H.E.*, vi. 12, 3): ἡμεῖς καὶ Πέτρον καὶ τοὺς ἄλλους ἀπόστολους ἀποδεχόμεθα ὡς Χριστόν,[3] could certainly have been also said a hundred years earlier. Already, in Gal. iv. 14, we read: ἐδέξασθέ με ὡς Χριστὸν Ιησοῦν. "The choice and sending out of the Apostles (after the Resurrection)" found its way even into the Rules of Faith,[4] and we may say that simply by an accident of history it did not find a place in the ancient Roman Symbol. Passages from prophecy were alleged as foretelling it just as in the case of main incidents in the life of Jesus Himself.[5] Writers in Asia Minor, Rome, and Egypt (before A.D. 160) unite in their testimony on this point, and even the Gnostics shared in part this conception.[6]

[1] Rev. xxi. 14.

[2] *Polycarp ad Phil.*, vi. 3: καθὼς αὐτὸς ἐνετείλατο καὶ οἱ εὐαγγελισάμενοι ἡμᾶς ἀπόστολοι.

[3] (We receive both Peter and the other Apostles as Christ.)

[4] Ascens. Isaiæ, iii. 13, ed Dillmann.

[5] Justin, *Apol.*, i. 39; Aristides, *Apol.*, 2.

[6] Jude 17; 2 Peter iii. 2; 1 Clem. 42; Barnab. v. 9; viii. 3; Didache, the title (Διδαχὴ κυρίου διὰ τῶν ιβ' ἀποστόλων!); Hermas, *Vis.*, iii. 5, *Sim.*, ix. 15, 16, 17, 25; Gospel of Peter; Apocalypse of Peter; Prædic. Petri in Clemens Alex., *Strom.*, vi. 6, 48; Ignat., ad Trall., 3; ad Rom., 4; ad Philad., 5; Papias; Polyc.; Aristides; Justin in many places; inferences from the great work of Irenæus; from the works of Tertullian and Clement of Alexandria; Valentinians (Ptolemy).

Everywhere the form in which the appeal to the Apostles, as the College of the Twelve, is couched proves that the idea in question was axiomatic. In my *Lehrbuch der Dogmengeschichte*, 1[4], S. 179–184, and elsewhere, I have more fully investigated the origin and the significance of this court of appeal, second to and yet one with Christ, which now at once became the vessel that received "Tradition" into itself.

Tradition always means the need of the present appealing to the authority of the past. In this case, however, an additional multitude of ideal and historical elements came into play.[1] Moreover the conflict with the Gnostics and the Marcionites must have thrust the absolute authority of the Twelve Apostles more and more into the foreground as against the claim of these opponents to a secret tradition, or their preference for one particular Apostle. Where one spoke of the Lord or of the

[1] He who wishes to know more about these elements must above all read Tertullian's treatise, *De Præsc. Heret.* "*Ecclesia*," and the idealised *Apostoli* are the central ideas of this treatise, and in them Jesus Christ is as it were enshrined. How could one then carry on with Gospels only as Holy Scripture! Without the addition of the second part to the new Canon there was no authentic document for the Church. "Qui acta apostolorum non receperunt," exclaims Tertullian, chap. xxii., "*nec spiritus sancti esse possunt*, (ut) qui necdum spiritum sanctum possunt agnoscere discentibus missum, sed nec ecclesiam se dicant defendere, qui quando et quibus incunabulis institutum est hoc corpus probare non habent." The Holy Spirit and the Apostles became correlative conceptions, with the consequence that the Scriptures of the New Testament were indifferently regarded as composed by the Holy Spirit or the Apostles.

Gospel, one might without irreverence add the Apostles, even in the case of the Gospels, since these took the place of the *Word* of the Lord. The formula, "The Books and the Apostles," is first met with in the so-called Second Epistle of Clement (chap. xiv. 2): *οὐκ οἴομαι ὑμᾶς ἀγνοεῖν ὅτι τὰ βιβλία καὶ οἱ ἀπόστολοι τὴν ἐκκλησίαν οὐ νῦν εἶναι ἀλλὰ ἄνωθεν (λέγουσιν).*[1] If *τὰ βιβλία* means the Scriptures of the Old Testament and the Gospels, then we have here a formula already very similar to that of the Scilitan martyrs ("libri et epistolæ Pauli viri justi," *vide infra*), and the same is the case if *τὰ βιβλία* means only the Gospels. If, however, by *τά βιβλία* the Old Testament alone is meant, then the Gospels and the Apostolus are included in the one term *οἱ ἀπόστολοι*, and this is the terminology that is also found in the Muratorian Fragment (lines 79 f.). But even if the author is supposed to be referring here to oral utterances of the Apostles—which is not probable because he seems to have a passage of Ephesians in his eye—the fact still remains that now "the Apostles" are placed in the same close connection with "the Scriptures" as some decades previously "the Scriptures" with "the Lord." Actual *writings* of the Twelve Apostles must have been sought for with ever more yearning and longing eyes. But

[1] (I do not suppose that you are ignorant that the Books and the Apostles [say] that the Church is not of this world but from above.)

were they to be found? One had indeed two Epistles of John, an Apocalypse of John, one of Peter, an Epistle of Jude that could be regarded as Apostolic (*vide* Tertullian, *De Cultu*, i. 3), and perhaps an Epistle of Peter. Little, indeed, and moreover of purely individual import; and besides we do not know whether these writings were anywhere to be found collected together before A.D. 180. What one must have and had not was a book in which the acts and the teaching of *all* the Twelve Apostles were described. We can understand that, under these circumstances, notice was attracted by the book that, among all existing books, approached closest to this ideal—namely the Acts of the Apostles. But there is no evidence that this happened before about A.D. 175. We must therefore for the moment leave this book out of consideration. Thus there remained in fact only the Pauline Epistles: they were collected and were in circulation in many of the Churches. No doubt when one spoke of the "Apostolus" in the first three-quarters of the second century, one had these works especially, perhaps exclusively, in one's eye.

But how far could the Lord be said to continue Himself in St Paul? This Apostle was certainly not of the number of the Twelve Apostles! To answer this question fully it would be necessary to take a wide outlook and to describe the history of the relation of St Paul to the original Apostles and the strict Jewish Christians. But it is sufficient to point out that the position which St Paul claimed and acquired in the Apostolic Age, and authenticated by his work, was one that allowed the Churches no vacillation and no compromise in their judgment. Here, indeed, it was true that "He that is not with me is against me." One was compelled either to acknowledge Paul as an Apostle of equal rank with the Twelve or to reject him as an interloper. And yet now—after he had long been recognised and after his epistles had increased in importance, because they alone gave clear expression to the theory of the New Covenant, which more and more gained ground—his equality with the Twelve seemed to be again in question; for, seeing that he was not an eye-witness of the life of the Lord, he could not testify to the facts of His history and His nature. In addition, the confident appeal of the Marcionites and Gnostics to the Apostle must have made Churchmen nervous.[1] But the custom of *public reading of the Pauline Epistles was already far too widely spread* and the prestige of the "righteous," the "good" Apostle, the "vas electionis" was already too firmly established to receive any real shock. Besides, it was possible to legitimise Paul by means of the Twelve Apostles as they were legitimised by Christ. They had indeed recognised

[1] Tertullian actually permits himself to speak of St Paul naturally ironically as "apostolus hereticorum."

him as an Apostle! Such legitimisation was by no means in the sense of St Paul himself; but this point was left out of consideration. According to the theory of succession, universally accepted at that time, he to whom office was delegated was of equal authority with him that conferred the office. Thus the equation held good: God=Christ=the Twelve Apostles=Paul. But where was to be found documentary evidence of Paul's legitimisation by the Twelve? In the Epistle to the Galatians; but that was not enough; the chapter in question could even be understood otherwise, and, besides, testimony which one gives to oneself is not trustworthy.[1] *The required testimony stood in the Acts of the Apostles.* This fact lent the book incomparable value; there was none like it, for, without it, the "Apostle" Paul with his epistles, regarded from the standpoint of strict tradition, was left in the air; while founded upon this book his epistles were "Apostolical" in the strictest sense of the word, and he himself stood as near to Christ as did the Twelve.

(*B*) We have already passed on to the subject of Attestation. In the history of any of the higher

[1] Tertullian, *De Præscrip.*, 23: "Possum et hic acta apostolorum repudiantibus dicere: prius est ut ostendatis quis iste Paulus et quid ante apostolum, et quomodo apostolus, quatenus et alias (scil. hæretici) ad quæstiones plurimum eo utantur. Neque enim si ipse se apostolum de persecutore profitetur, sufficit unicuique examinate credenti, quando nec dominus ipse de se testimonium dixerit."

religions, of those at least which depend upon demonstration and proof, there comes a moment—and that soon—when *attestation* becomes as important as *content*. If the adherents of a "*new*" *religion* present its content as identical with that of original religion, all that they have to do is simply to disperse the obscurity into which original religion has fallen among men. If, then, the new religion contains doctrinal statements that are adapted to this purpose, it is only necessary to prove their *trustworthiness* and all is accomplished. Such was the method of the Apologists when face to face with the heathen: their chief task was to prove the trustworthiness of the prophets who accompanied history with a long chain of witness. If the demonstration proved irrefutable, the religion was justified. Soon the same method came to the front in internal controversies among Christians. When once the history of the *Kurios Christus*, His Divinity and Humanity, came to occupy the centre of interest—and this already happened in the Apostolic Age—everything depended upon *attestation*; for the content of the message was by no means so strange to the heathen. It was not the essence of the message, "the manifested God," that they felt to be "folly," but its accidents, and that the "Mythus" was not to be regarded as merely symbolic, but as actual history. All attestation of historical facts is carried out by an unbroken chain of παραδιδόναι (on the part of those who are authorised) and of παραλαμβάνεσθαι. Following up the chain, the Twelve Apostles and no others could rank as the ultimate authorities for the tradition! If the content of the tradition became a matter of controversy it was necessary to find one's way back to them, just as in the case of the message concerning God the Creator it was necessary to find one's way to Abraham, Noah, and Adam. If it was necessary in the latter case to prove that Homer and the other Greeks were "later," and therefore without authority, so here one must prove the same of the Gnostic teachers together with the supposed Apostolic authorities to which they appealed. With this intention, Papias made earnest and exclusive inquiry after what the Twelve Apostles had said (apart from the Gospels) concerning Christ,[1] and Justin presented the Gospels, even to his heathen readers—thus not to Gnostics—as *memorabilia* of the *Apostles*[2]; as indeed Papias before him doubtless assigned the highest value to this character of the Gospels upon which he based his great work concerning Christ. Gospels, therefore, which bore the name of an Apostle or a

[1] Euseb., *H.E.*, iii. 39. These inquiries, however, do not appear to have been very fruitful, and their results seem to have been of very questionable value.

[2] In many passages. To the Jews he presented the Johannine Apocalypse, not as the work of a Christian prophet, but as the work of an Apostle of Christ (*Dial.*, 81).

disciple of the Apostles[1] acquired a new attribute: they were not only "Scriptures of the Lord," but also "Apostolic Scriptures," and gradually it came to be as important that they were the latter as it was that they were the former. If, however, the Gospels as *Apostolic* writings became so important because of their *attesting* power, it follows that every Apostolic writing must have become important because it could "give attestation." Accordingly Epistles and Apocalypses, if they were Apostolic, appear in a new light. Not only their rich and various content and their aim gave them a considerable value, but they acquired a yet higher value from their origin as *Apostolic* works. We know that in Rome at the end of the second century all the writings of the New Testament were subsumed under the one title "Apostoli," just as the Scriptures of the Old Testament were simply called "prophetæ" (*vide supra* the Muratorian Fragment); indeed that, perhaps, at the time of the Second Epistle of Clement, "Apostles" was already the designation for both Epistles and Gospels. When, however, this simple distinction between the new and the old collection, expressed in the term

[1] Tert., *De Præsc.*, 32: "Sicut apostoli non diversa inter se docuisserin, ita apostolici non contraria apostolis edidissent"; *Advers. Marc.*, iv. 2, 5: "Nobis fidem ex apostolis Ioannes et Matthæus insinuant, ex apostolicis Lucas et Marcus instaurant, iisdem regulis exorsi . . . Marcus quod edidit (evangelium) Petri adfirmetur, cuius interpres Marcus. Nam et Lucæ digestum Paulo adscribere solent. Capit magistrorum videri quæ discipuli promulgarint."

"Prophetæ-Apostoli,"[1] had once been worked out and thoroughly settled by the Montanist controversy, then first the "Apostolic" shone forth in full glory; indeed even the words of the Lord appear now only as jewels in the monstrance of the *traditio et doctrina apostolica* which included all—even Gospels with the Kurios—and, in itself, expressed all that God after the time of the Old Testament had granted to mankind. *The division of the new collection into two parts is secondary when compared with its unity; but this unity bears on its forefront the title "the Apostles," not "the Lord."* What a swing round!

(*C*) But must not the formal addition of the Pauline Epistles, as they stood and as they were read, to the growing new Canon have presented continual difficulties? When we consider much of their content we may well suppose that this was so. Did they then come into the Canon *faute de mieux* or because, under the dominance of the idea of the Apostolic, ever growing in importance, the custom of public reading insensibly attached them to the Canon? Neither of these explanations is in my opinion sufficient, rather we must again take into account the canonical collections of Marcion and the Gnostics. We have already had recourse to these in answering the question how a second Canon arose in

[1] In spite of the distinction "Prophetæ-Apostoli," it was still assumed that the Apostles had also the prophetic character as an addition to the Apostolate; but so far as I know they are never simply called "Prophets."

the Church. Now we must inquire whether they were not also of influence in the division of this second Canon into two parts and in determining the important position that St Paul occupies in it.

Marcion's Canon was twofold: it comprised the Gospels and ten Pauline Epistles. The twofold paradox of the New Testament of the Church that it is twofold, and that the Pauline Epistles form so large a part of the second division, is thus foreshadowed in Marcion's Canon. But it is also foreshadowed in the Valentinian Canon, as we may conclude from Ptolemy's letter to Flora.[1] In those heretical circles the reverence for St Paul was almost boundless. Origen tells us that according to the Marcionites St Paul sat on the right hand of Christ in heaven—as Christ sits on the right hand of the Father. Marcionites, among whom the Johannine Gospel had partly come into favour, or some other heretics, declared that he was the promised Paraclete.[2] It was, moreover, Marcion himself that,

[1] There is no certain ground for the assumption that the Valentinians possessed any other writings in their Canon besides Gospels and Pauline Epistles. As for the Acts of the Apostles, Tertullian (*De Præsc.*, 22), says that the heretics rejected it.

[2] Orig., in Lucam Hom., 25 (iii. p. 962*b*): "Denique in tantam quidem dilectionis audaciam proruperunt Marcionitæ, ut nova quædam et inaudita super Paulo monstra confingerent. Aiunt enim, hoc quod scriptum est, sedere a dextris salvatoris et sinistris de Paulo et de Marcione dici, quod Paulus sedet a dextris, Marcion sedet a sinistris. Porro alii legentes: 'Mittam vobis advocatum spiritum veritatis' nolunt intelligere tertiam personam a patre et filio, sed apostolum Paulum."

according to Esnik, taught that Christ had twice descended from Heaven; the first time to suffer and to die, the second time to call Paul and *to reveal first to him the significance of His death.*[1] The bipartite division of the new Canon into "Gospel and Paul" was accordingly for Marcion a matter of course.

Could this fact have influenced the great Churches? I believe that we may well assume that it did. Were the great Churches to lag behind the heretics in reverence for St Paul? This would have meant, as things lay—*i.e.* it must be either one thing or the other—the surrender to them of Paul. But it appears that we also have external evidence for our assumption. We have indeed long known that Marcionite readings found their way into the ecclesiastical text of the Pauline Epistles, but now for seven years we have known that Churches actually accepted the Marcionite prefaces to the Pauline Epistles! De Bruyne has made one of the finest discoveries of later days in proving that those prefaces, which we read first in *Codex*

[1] Esnik (*vide* my *Lehrbuch d. Dogmengeschichte*, 1[4], S. 304): "Then the second time Jesus descended in the form of His Godhead to the Lord of created things (the Demiurge) and held judgment with him concerning His death. . . . Then He left him and caught up Paul and showed him the price, and sent him to preach concerning the price for which we were bought, and that all that believe in Jesus are bought back from this righteous (God) to the good (God)." Thus Paul was the first to reveal the secret of redemption, not Jesus Himself.

Fuldensis and then in numbers of later manuscripts, are Marcionite, and that the Churches had not noticed the cloven hoof.[1] But this proves only the influence of the text! No, it shows the influence of the *Marcionite collection of the epistles upon the formation of the ecclesiastical collection.* Are we then to suppose that it had no influence upon the *idea* of the collection itself as set side by side with the Gospels? Surely we may assume that this influence upon the formation of the collection goes back to a very early period. Does not this lead us back to the time of the origin of the ecclesiastical Canon? But, even if we are sceptical in regard to this piece of external testimony, it still remains true as we previously stated that what was an accomplished fact with the Marcionites and the Valentinians could not have remained without significance for the Churches.

There is, besides, another point to be considered. It is true that the speculation advanced by the author of the Muratorian Fragment[2]—that Paul like John, in that he wrote letters to *seven* Churches, wrote really to *one,* thus to the universal Church—was certainly first imagined at a time when the Epistles had already found their place in the Canon, and when it was wished to justify the inclusion

[1] "Prologues bibliques d'origine Marcionite" (Rev. Bénéd., 1907, Januar., p. 1–16), also *Theol. Ztg.*, 1907, No. 5. *Vide* the copy of the prefaces in our first Appendix.

[2] And, we may say, countless others after him.

there of such occasional writings.[1] But the idea, "Apostolus ad omnes scripsit dum ad quosdam,"[2] is naturally much earlier in date. It must have made its appearance wherever men had learned to value the edifying power of the Epistles. The "catholicity" of the Epistles was clear from many passages that they contained; and even if there had been fewer passages whose general ecclesiastical importance was not of itself conspicuous and needed no artificial light, yet the Apostolus belongs to the Ecclesia and the Ecclesia to the Apostolus! When once the concept and title Apostle had been given to St Paul it could only be a question of time when his writings, whatever they contained, would be formally elevated to the plane of "ecclesiastical" Scripture. That herein the real service, which some of his Epistles had always contributed and still continued to contribute to the cause of Church order, played a certain *rôle* is shown by the quaint little note of the Muratorian Fragment in reference to St Paul's Epistles to particular persons: "In ordinatione ecclesiasticæ disciplinæ sanctificatæ sunt."

But St Paul could never be "*the* Apostolus." He could not give *direct testimony*; and certain objectionable elements, presented by the particular and occasional character and peculiarities of his Epistles

[1] If St Paul had happened to write to three or ten Churches instead of to seven, we may be certain that the Universal Church would have been found to have been suggested by the number.

[2] Tert., *Advers. Marc.*, v. 17.

and hindering their formal canonisation, remained a difficulty.[1] This is the reason why, only twenty years before Tertullian's famous statement concerning the Bible of the Roman Church—and therefore also of the African Church—(" Ecclesia Romana legem et prophetas cum evangelicis et apostolicis litteris miscit ; [2] inde potat fidem," *De Præsc.*, 36), African Christians, laymen, as it seems, answered the question : " Quæ sunt res in capsa vestra ? " with the words : " Libri et epistulæ Pauli viri iusti." We learn that at this time in Africa the Epistles of St Paul had a place beside the sacred collection, but that the last step, by which they became fully identified with the *γραφαί*, had not yet been taken. Here we actually see into the process of growth of the New Testament, and that directly before its final close.[3] The distinction between the " Scriptures " and Paul is still

[1] As was felt even in the fourth and fifth centuries by the more sober theologians of the Antiochean school.

[2] Cf. *De Baptism,* 15 : " Tam ex domini evangelio quam ex apostoli litteris." It has been even conjectured that the bipartite division of the Old Testament (" Lex et Prophetæ ") influenced the similar division of the New Testament ; but this cannot be proved nor is it even probable, seeing that the bipartite division can be fully explained otherwise, and that the relation of " Evangelium " and " Apostolus " can be compared with that of " Law " and " Prophets " only in one aspect, while in others the parallel fails.

[3] The very peculiar formula of Tertullian : "Instrumenta divinarum rerum et sanctorum Christianorum " (*De Præsc.*, 40), seems to give us another glimpse into the growth of the new Canon. But we cannot be sure what Tertullian means by " instrumenta sanctorum Christianorum."

found in the controversial work of the Roman Caius (about A.D. 200).

The Pauline Epistles, because they were widely read, at the very beginning came as it were into Court with the claim to be constituents of the New Testament that was to be; but it was only after a slow process that they won a place beside the Canonical Scriptures, and only because of this slow process were they able to obtain and maintain a place in the Canon and finally to form its second division. But in this second division there also stood, as we learn from Irenæus, the Muratorian Fragment and Tertullian—about A.D. 180–200—that is, as soon as the Second Canon was in existence—at least 5 (6) other works: The Acts of the Apostles, two Johannine epistles, Revelation, the Epistle of Jude, and perhaps 1 Peter.[1] Concerning the last five works, we may be sure that wherever they were in circulation they would at once have been added to the new Canon as apostolic works in the strict sense of the word. Search was evidently

[1] Polycarp, in his epistle, uses this work but does not quote it, treating it just as he does 1 Clement, while he deals otherwise with the Pauline Epistles. It is wanting in the Muratorian Fragment, and Tertullian in his earlier works does not quote it (yet it is different with Irenæus). The questions therefore arise whether Peter was regarded as the author of the work, and whether it belonged to the most ancient form of the Canon. I therefore neglect it. We may, however, assume that the Apocalypse of Peter belonged at first to the Canon, but that in Rome *very soon* it was objected to (*vide* the Muratorian Fragment. More will be said below concerning this question and the case of the Shepherd of Hermas).

made for such writings, which were indeed just the kind of works that were needed for the second division of the Canon; and, therefore, even a little fugitive piece like the Epistle of Jude was accepted seeing that one could regard its author as an Apostle.[1] How unfortunate that so few works of the Twelve Apostles could be found and then each only giving the testimony of *one* Apostle! Where could a book be found that gave the testimony of all the Apostles and reproduced their teaching? The Acts of the Apostles was at once seized upon. We have already (p. 53) spoken of this book; we shall now consider it in greater detail. It did not, indeed, offer all that could be wished in accordance with the idea that governed the development of the new Canon, yet what it offered was of extraordinary importance. *It stood forth as the grand fundamental document of what was primitive and apostolic and of the testimony which was now all important.* From the standpoint of the early Catholic time it possessed the following advantages:

1. It was the work of that Luke who, by his work that stood in the Canon of the Gospels, was already recognised as "vir apostolicus" and a Canonical author.[2]

[1] Tertullian expressly gives him the title (*De Cultu*, i. 3 "[Scriptura] Enoch apud Judam apostolum testimonium possidet").

[2] It is true that this is not brought out in the title which was given to the book. But Irenæus, the Muratorian Fragment, and Tertullian lay emphasis upon this point. Reflection upon the content of the book was the more important element in the composition of the title.

2. It described the early history of the Church in an heroic style—*i.e.* it bore testimony to the classical character of that history.

3. It reported speeches and testimonies of *all* the Apostles by the mouth of St Peter.

4. It related the missionary activity of at least one, if not two, of the primitive Apostles, an activity that could be regarded as the *work of all the Apostles.*

5. It described the transition from the mission to the Jews to the mission to the Gentiles, showing that it was carried out by St Peter and by the decision of the Primitive Community.

6. It legitimised St Paul (in the sense of full Apostolate), both himself and the content of his teaching, and it afforded highly desirable lines of direction for the interpretation of "difficult" passages in the Pauline Epistles according to the *communis opinio* of the Church.

That the book was seen in the light of these advantages is clearly proved by the statements of Irenæus and Tertullian. With the former, St Paul and his Epistles stand simply under the defensive shadow of the Acts; their authority in history and in the Canon appears guaranteed simply by this book. Nor is it otherwise with Tertullian in passages of decisive importance.[1] Irenæus boldly

[1] Vide *De Præscs.*, 22, 23; *Advers. Marc.*, i. 20; iv. 2–5; v. 1–3. *Cf.* also the passages quoted above, p. 49, note, p. 53, note.

states (iii. 14, 1) that Luke was "non solum prosecutor sed et co-operarius *apostolorum*" (adding "maxime autem Pauli" in order to reconcile somewhat his extravagant statement with actual history). Further, the author of the Muratorian Fragment introduced the work with the audacious title: "Acta *omnium* apostolorum,"[1] and Tertullian roundly asserts: "Qui Acta Apostolorum non recipiunt nec spiritus sancti esse possunt." Here we see clearly in what high estimation the book stood, what was desired of it, and with what determined purpose it was made the most of *by inserting it between the Gospels and the Pauline Epistles.* And yet we must recognise that according to the testimony of Tertullian the book did not stand in the Canon of the Gnostics, that the Eucratites also rejected it,[2] that before the time of Irenæus and the Muratorian Fragment there is not even a shred of evidence that it was used in public lection or had any aspirations in the direction of inclusion in the growing Canon;[3] finally, that the book was not of a kind that from any point of view would entitle it to be included in a collection of authoritative works, under circumstances

[1] Even the title Πράξεις τῶν ἀποστόλων in the Canon claims much too much.

[2] Euseb., *H.E.*, iv. 30, 5: μὴ τὰς Πράξεις τῶν Ἀποστόλων καταδεχόμενοι.

[3] We have no knowledge, or as good as no knowledge, of the Acts before it makes its appearance in the New Testament.

as they existed between the years A.D. 70 and 170. Taking all these points into consideration, we must conclude *that the placing of this book in the growing Canon shows evidence of reflection, of conscious purpose, of a strong hand acting with authority; and that by such conscious action the ideal Canon, in outline at least, was realised in the form of the bipartite New Testament both Apostolic and Catholic.*

The small collection of Apostolic-Catholic epistles took its place in the Canon by a process parallel to that of the Acts. In the Canon they both serve the same aim; the former, as it were, by their own inborn right—yet to a limited extent because they were so few and so short; the Acts, however, was thrust into its position, and, rightly exploited, could fulfil the aim in a high degree.

The Acts is in a certain way the key to the understanding of the idea of the New Testament of the Church, and has given it the organic structure in which it stands before us. By taking its place at the head of the " Apostolus " the Acts first made possible the division of the Canon into two parts and justified the combination of the Pauline Epistles with the Gospels. It is also possible to speak of a threefold division, in which the Acts (together with the Catholic Epistles and Revelation) formed the central portion.

The Acts of the Apostles proves that the New Testament is " late," *i.e.* that in its form it belongs to a period not earlier than the end of the second century. So far as its constituent works are concerned it is earlier, for these for a considerable time had been used in public lection (even if not regularly) and the Gospels for decades had held a position close to, and of equal prestige with, the Old Testament. Hence the transition from the earlier condition of things to the "New Testament" was for many Churches scarcely noticeable.

§ 3. *Why does the New Testament contain Four Gospels and not One only?*

The original title of the Gospels in the Canon had the following form :

The Gospel { according to Matthew.
according to Mark.
according to Luke.
according to John.

So run the most ancient authorities (the word Gospel is not repeated). Casual reflection tells us that titles so completely similar and at the same time so imperfect cannot proceed from the authors themselves. We must conclude that these titles, like the title Πράξεις τῶν ἀποστόλων, have been added at a later date. Thus the original titles have been lost or rather have been deleted ; for these works must have borne titles.

Yet we can trace these titles back to the middle of the second century. This fact and the similarity of their form make it certain that they proceed from the person who first brought together these four books and bound them in one. Consequently this did not happen (as in the case of the Acts) when the twofold New Testament took form, but at an earlier date.[1]

In the Manuscripts the *common* title for all four Gospels is "The Gospel." The compiler did not unintentionally not repeat the word "Gospel" in the title to each individual Gospel. They were intended in combination to present "The Gospel"; none of them had the right by itself to be called "The Gospel." Still less might one speak of the Gospel "of Matthew," etc; for the word Evangelium had its own self-evident genitive, "Jesu Christi."

Nor, on the other hand, may we take these titles "according to Matthew," etc., as if by them the compiler would imply that these books were not composed by Matthew, etc., but were only indirectly dependent upon these men. No one in antiquity understood the titles in this way. The matter becomes quite clear when we consider the titles of the apocryphal Gospels: The Gospel of Peter professes to be written by St

[1] If it had happened shortly before the year A.D. 200 we may well conjecture that care would have been taken that in the titles St Mark should appear as the Gospel of Peter, St Luke as the Gospel of Paul.

Peter, for St Peter speaks in the first person, and yet this Gospel bears the title: "The Gospel according to Peter." The titles Κατὰ Ματθαῖον, etc., mean "The Gospel according to Matthew's own description," etc., *not* "The Gospel according to Matthew's tradition," etc.[1]

The character and the similarity of the titles shows that the four books were intended to be regarded as *one* work in fourfold presentation. Irenæus so conceives it when he speaks of the "four-formed" Gospel,[2] and the view finds especially clear expression in the Muratorian Fragment, the author of which with circumstantiality, but most significantly, writes: "The third book of the Gospel according to Luke," "The fourth book of the Gospel according to John." The compiler of these four books thus judged them not as works important in the first place (or even at all) because of their authors, nor even as works each of which by itself fulfilled the object which each had in view—for then he would not have given us four of them—nor even as "Gospels" (as if there could have been several Gospels), but as books which together presented the Gospel. In them was contained all that

[1] There were also gospels called καθ' Ἑβραίους and κατ' Αἰγυπτίους. Here κατά can only mean "according to the use of" or something similar. We do not know the origin of these terms. But it seems that they are connected with one another—that in Egypt the gospel used by Jewish Christians had the one name and the gospel used by Gentile Christians had the other.

[2] iii. 11. 8.

could be known and was to be known about the Gospel.

This condition of things can be traced back for Asia Minor to the time of Irenæus' earliest youth, *i.e.* to just before the middle of the second century. Irenæus has no conception that the written Gospel ever existed otherwise than in this form; indeed he ascribes its fourfold form to a Divine dispensation which answered to the dispensation of Nature, and which was already foreshadowed in the Old Testament.[1]

Nor is it by pure accident that through the testimony of Irenæus we are able to say that in Asia Minor this condition of things existed before the middle of the second century; for as I have shown in my *Chronologie*, i. S. 589 ff., 681–701, it is most probable that the compilation of our four Gospels took place in Asia Minor, and that from thence the εὐαγγέλιον τετράμορφον[2] started on its victorious course in connection with the anti-Gnostic controversies, and in some few decades established itself in most of the provincial Churches.

We know that long before the middle of the second century, in fact, already at the time of John the Presbyter, there was much discussion concerning the Four Gospels, which were confronted and compared with one another, and that in these discussions *John himself played an authoritative part.*

[1] iii. 11. 8; iii. 1. [2] (Fourfold Gospel.)

These discussions turned, in the first place, upon questions of *completeness and the correct order of events* in the respective Gospels, and also upon questions as to whether the authors were *eye-witnesses*, and whether *in their works they had given a duly lofty expression to the nature of Christ.*[1] As usually happens in such controversies, some took up an exclusive standpoint and accepted only the Johannine Gospel or, on the other hand, only the Synoptic Gospels (or even only one of these ?), alleging that the other Gospels had no authority, and even attempting to convict them of heresy. The result of these discussions and controversies was that neither the Synoptics nor "John" were dispensed with, but that they were all set together in one compilation in the way that has been above mentioned.[2] The compilation was thus evidently

[1] The evidence—all pointing to Asia Minor—is found in Papias, Clement of Alexandria, the Muratorian Fragment, Hippolytus—Epiphanius (Alogi), and Euseb., *H.E.*, iii. 24.

[2] This meant, whether it was intended or not, that chief prestige was assigned to the fourth Gospel; for this Gospel could, indeed, be rejected, but once accepted its superiority was therewith silently admitted. With this Gospel—and here I agree with Overbeck in the work quoted above—it was a case of "Thou shalt have none other gods but me." We may at the same time allow that its author—like the Presbyter in regard to Mark—could respect the other Gospels as right worthy performances, and could even champion them from this point of view; but he certainly did not wish to see them at his side. (Jülicher *Einl.*[5], S. 465, says that St John did not mean to replace St Matthew and St Luke. Certainly, he had quite different aims in writing his book; but did he intend that his book should be placed side by side with those Gospels ? And may it not be that the purpose to supplant them is not obvious in his work because it

a compromise, not between Jewish and Gentile Christians—this controversy did not even come into consideration—but between usages and conflicting traditions in the chief Churches of Asia Minor, especially Ephesus, concerning Gospels to be read at public worship, traditions that originated in perhaps Achaia (St Luke), in Palestine (St Matthew), in Rome (St Mark), and in Asia Minor itself (St John).[1] I would just remark that owing to the meeting together of several Gospels in one neighbourhood the Churches for a time were led to exercise a kind of historical criticism upon them (concerning such points as the completeness, the correctness of the

was assumed as a matter of course ?). Again the third Gospel also was intended to be *the* Gospel, and Eusebius (who certainly knew Greek !) is surely right when he understands from the prologue that St Luke was not satisfied with his predecessors, and so not even with St Mark, and regarded their works as rather presumptuous (*H.E.*, iii. 24, 15). Further, the formal style of the introduction to St Mark shows that the author meant this work to be *the* story, not one among many stories. Finally, both these Gospels, in spite of the high claims they make for themselves, do not anywhere show that they were intended for public reading ; while St Matthew evidently was from the first so intended. I have no doubt that the two other Synoptic Gospels obtained the rank and dignity of works to be read in the Church, just because they were associated with St Matthew (*vide* my *Neue Unters. zur Apostelgeschichte*, 1911, S. 94).

[1] Just as we must in this connection completely disregard the earlier controversy between Jewish and Gentile Christians, so also we must reject the hypothesis that any one, except Marcion, ever noticed theological differences between the Synoptic Gospels. A controversy, however, certainly existed in Asia Minor between these and the Johannine Gospel as to whether they depended upon eye-witnesses, and concerning the correctness and theological content of their records.

order of events, the conception of the Person of Christ); and that, accordingly, for a few decades, the Church in Asia Minor adopted an attitude towards the Gospels which she never allowed herself to adopt in the following centuries.

The compromise took place under the sign of the Johannine Gospel. Those who would have this late book read in the Churches of Asia Minor carried their point against the "Alogi"; but as they were not able to abolish the earlier tradition in regard to public lection there arose the difficulty of a plurality of Gospels. If it had been a question of only two Gospels the difficulty would have been great enough, it could scarcely have been increased when it was a question of three or four. Indeed, we may conjecture that the situation created by the success of the fourth Gospel made it possible for all three Synoptics to remain as Gospel books of the Church side by side with the Johannine Gospel, instead of, perhaps, St Matthew only, or only St Mark and St Luke; and for existing usages, apart from that of the Johannine Gospel, to be tolerated rather than repressed.

But at the time that this fourfold work was compiled, did its author really mean it to be the last word, or was it to be regarded as only provisional? In my *Reden und Aufsätzen* (ii. S. 239 ff.) I have given some reasons for regarding the latter alternative as very probable. Jülicher (*loc.*

cit.) is of contrary opinion, and asserts that "there was no more need that one should object to four Gospels than to thirteen Pauline Epistles, or to parallel accounts of incidents in Old Testament history. The differences were not felt, one only rejoiced at the confirmation which each new evangelist afforded to the other, and in the last resort one had recourse to the obvious theory that the later evangelist completed the record of the earlier. Naturally every small sect had its *one* Gospel; just as naturally in the Catholic Church spread over three continents different books for a time divided this prestige, and then settled down peacefully together."

In my opinion these remarks of Jülicher do not reflect the feelings and circumstances of that period. Is it really true that at that period four Gospels must have been just as unobjectionable as thirteen Pauline Epistles?—to say nothing of the fact that, as is proved by the Muratorian Fragment, even the thirteen Pauline Epistles were not felt to be absolutely unobjectionable. It is surely of the essence of an *authoritative* history that it should be *one* and that its prestige should be felt to be in peril if other accounts are set side by side with it.[1] Still more if this history was

[1] The comparison with double accounts in the Old Testament does not hold good; for we do not know what difficulties they caused during the process of canonisation in the Synagogue. The Church here had no choice; she simply had to accept the Canon with its difficulties.

meant to be read regularly at public worship, alternative readings from other accounts must have led to serious misunderstandings. Jülicher's comparison with "Epistles" is surely out of place. It was only the special address of the epistles that caused certain difficulties; apart from this there could have been as many epistles as there were psalms without causing any trouble. Neither is it true that no one took offence at the plurality of Gospels or felt the differences in their accounts. Did not the very author of the Muratorian Fragment write: "Licet varia singulis evangeliorum libris principia doceantur, nihil tamen differt credentium fidei, cum uno ac principali spiritu declarata sint in omnibus omnia de nativitate, de passione, de resurrectione, etc."? This is said in opposition to objections which were founded on the plurality of Gospels in itself and on the differences in their accounts, among which differences *one* is emphasised as an especially important example! And is not the whole discussion of the question by Irenæus (iii. 11. 9) an apology for *four* Gospels in face of the natural demand for only *one*? He also is compelled to make play with the ἑνὶ πνεύματι συνεχόμενον[1] against the τετράμορφον[2] (a term which in itself only smooths over the actual difficulty)—an argument which could have given little real satisfaction; and following upon him and the

[1] (Held together by one Spirit.) [2] (Fourfold.)

author of the Muratorian Fragment constant attempts were made in the Church to force the troublesome plurality into an artificial unity. "The differences were not felt," says Jülicher. Surely it is just the contrary: from the two different genealogies of Jesus to the accounts of His appearances after His Resurrection the differences in the Gospels were most acutely felt, and all kinds of attempts were made to harmonise them—think only of Julius Africanus for one! Nor can I find scarcely anywhere evidence that "one rejoiced at the confirmation that the new evangelist afforded to the other." What "confirmation" was needed by an evangelist who had the name Matthew or Mark? Moreover, "the obvious theory that the later evangelist completed the account of the earlier," described by Jülicher as a "last resort," not only contradicted the very idea of a Canonical Gospel, but first made its appearance at a comparatively late date, and certainly did not give pure joy. Finally, I must dissent from the suggestion that "if every small sect had its *one* Gospel just as naturally in the Catholic Church spread over three continents, *different* books for a time divided this prestige and then settled down peacefully together." Here the contrast between "small sect" and "Catholic Church" seems to be incorrectly drawn: on this point the needs of the Catholic Church could not have been other than those of the smallest sect. Moreover, all separated Christian communities (not only small sects) of which we have knowledge, except those that separated themselves from the Catholic Church after the creation of the Canon of four Gospels, had only *one* Gospel: for instance, the Jewish Christians in Palestine and Egypt, the early Gentile Christians of Egypt, the Marcionite Church throughout the world, the Gnostic Jewish Christians, and those Christians of Asia Minor that rejected the Synoptic Gospels. The plurality of the Gospels was a peculiarity unique in character of which, to judge from the earliest Christian writings that quote "the Gospel" or Gospel material (1 Clement, Didache, etc.), no one then had the slightest conception.

We are therefore quite justified in our inquiry whether the concession that four Gospels were suitable for public lection, made in Asia Minor after stress and controversy, was intended as a final solution of the problem. The Marcan Gospel and the collection of sayings (*Q*), the author of which was probably the Apostle St Matthew, were followed by our St Luke and St Matthew, which were really "harmonies." In these two Gospels the two sources are worked up into single books without any regard to the dignity of their authors. Why should not the process have been continued to a further stage of unification, and the concession of four distinct Gospels have been regarded as only provisional? Even if we had no further information the question would not be superfluous; for it is suggested by the previous course of Gospel construction. But we are not without further information. It is true that the supposition, suggested by a series of indications, that so early a writer as Justin had recourse to a Gospel harmony in addition to the separate Gospels, cannot be regarded as sufficiently probable in spite of laborious attempts to prove it; but we know as a fact that Tatian composed a harmony of the four Gospels, and that in the East this work very soon obtained the widest circulation as "The Gospel." Evidently Tatian composed this work not for private purposes but, as the result shows, in order to replace "the Gospels of the separated." In these last days, von Soden, senior, and others with him, have asserted that this work must also have played an important *rôle* in the very early history of the Greco-Latin Churches, seeing that it has had an extraordinary influence upon the text of the Gospels in these Churches; but one can only say that this hypothesis still lacks confirmation. Still so much must be allowed—this book was not intended to be confined only to the Syrian Churches, it was meant to serve the Church as a whole, and in this intention it was not altogether unsuccessful. Again, we hear from St Jerome that Theophilus,

Bishop of Antioch, also composed a Gospel Harmony (about A.D. 180).[1] Unfortunately we have no knowledge of its details; still we may conclude that Theophilus, like Tatian, felt that the arrangement of four Gospels was something that was only provisional.

What, then, hindered the process of combining the four Gospels into *one*, not only in Asia Minor, but also in the Greco-Latin Churches; so that in spite of all the disadvantages of plurality they still remained distinct? The answer does not seem difficult. Here also the interest was at work that asserted itself so powerfully everywhere in the Church soon after the beginning of the second century—the interest in *testimony* (*vide supra*, pp. 54 ff.). This interest — *the interest in the Apostolic, in sure and certain tradition*—surpassed all other interests and triumphed over all objections. To possess records given by such persons as Matthew and John must have been more important to the Churches in conflict with Gnosticism than any other consideration.[2] We already see this in the case of Justin who, when he composed his apology, had already written at length against heretics.

[1] *Ep. ad Algasiam* (i. pp. 860 f. Valtarsi): "Theophilus, Antiochenæ ecclesiæ septimus post Petrum apostolum episcopus, qui *quattuor evangelistarum in unum corpus dicta compingens* ingenii sui nobis monumenta dimisit, etc."

[2] In this sense one also spoke of the *Διδαχὴ τοῦ κυρίου διὰ τῶν ιβ′ ἀποστόλων* and of *τῶν ἀποστόλων ὑμῶν ἐντολὴ τοῦ κυρίου καὶ σωτῆρος* (2 Pet. iii. 2).

Naturally the Gospels are to him important in the first place because they tell of the Lord ; yet they are to him almost as important, because they are " Memorabilia of the Apostles," and we have every reason to suppose that Papias, a somewhat earlier contemporary of Justin, was of the same opinion ; that with him, too, the apostolic names borne by the Gospels, declaring their apostolic origin, formed an instance of highest authority in the controversy with heretics concerning trustworthy knowledge of the person of Christ and of the evangelic history. Interest in testimony to tradition could not now allow the four Gospels to be combined into one ; for then the names would have been lost, or at least left uncertain. Hence all efforts in the direction of a Diatessaron had no longer any chance of success ; the Church was compelled to abide by the "four" and to see their unity, such as it was, in the *spiritus principalis* : The Gospel remained " tetramorphon " in the sense of " the separated." [1] *In principle the same interest as that which led to the formation of the second part of the New Testament (the Apostolus), also perpetuated the collection of four Gospels*, so that it never arrived at literary unity. In the name " Apostoli," which the author of the Muratorian Fragment uses for the *whole* Canon, this interest finds sharp expression.

[1] Lietzmann agrees in this view (*Wie wurden die B.B. der N.T. heilige Schrift?* 1907, S. 67).

Not only in the second division of the New Testament, but also in the fact that the Gospel is given in four books, we possess a lasting memorial of the Apostolic tradition that set itself on a level with the word and history of the Lord. This memorial was purchased at great cost, at the cost, indeed, of real sacrifice, for into the bargain came all the difficulties that four separate records must have created for public lection, for the instruction of catechumens, and for exegesis—difficulties which certainly at first must have appeared almost insurmountable.

The question set in the title of this paragraph is then to be answered as follows: The New Testament contains four Gospels and not only *one*, because at the beginning of the second century these four Gospels met together in Asia Minor (probably in Ephesus), and after controversy and conflict peaceably settled down together. From Asia Minor this arrangement passed to the other Churches.[1] In the background lay the purpose to

[1] As an indication that St Matthew was as yet little known, or altogether unknown in Rome at the beginning of the second century, we have also a piece of external evidence, though it is not certainly altogether clear, *vide* the note of Eusebius (pseudo-Eusebius) preserved in Syriac concerning the star of the Magi (Nestle, "*Marginalien u. Materialien*," S. 72; *cf.* my *Chronologie*, ii. S. 126): "In the second year of the coming of our Lord, under the consulate of Cæsar and Capito, in the month Kanun II., these Magi came from the East and worshipped our Lord. And in the year 430 (1st Oct. 118/9), in the reign of Hadrian, under the consulate of Severus and Fulgus [Fulvius] (A.D. 120), during the episcopate of Xystus, bishop of the

find some single form in which the Church might present what was contained in the four; but this purpose was very soon crossed by the perception that the four books *as works of Matthew and John, of Mark and Luke,* acquired in conflict with the false tradition of the Gnostics an importance immeasurable and irreplaceable. Therefore these *apostolic* works were allowed to remain separate in spite of all the difficulties which were thereby involved; and attempts like that of Tatian to bring the four into one—attempts which were in the line of previous development—found no acceptance in the Church.

§ 4. *Why has only* one *Apocalypse been able to keep its place in the New Testament? Why not several—or none at all?*

In answering this question [1] we may suitably take the Muratorian Fragment as our starting-point. At the close of its positive section occurs a paragraph which may be paraphrased as follows:

"We also accept Apocalypses, but only two, those of John and Peter; yet the latter is rejected by a minority among us. The Shepherd of Hermas

city of Rome, this question arose among people who were acquainted with Holy Scripture, and through the efforts of great men in different places this story was sought for and found and written in the language of those who cared for it."

[1] It has been already touched upon (pp. 35 f.), but requires more detailed discussion.

ought not to be spoken of as a part of the Canon either now or at any future time ; for it was written only lately in our own times in Rome under the Bishop Pius, the brother of the author ; our Canon can only contain *apostoli*. Neither ought it to be added to the Old Testament, as some wish who point to the prophetic character of the work ; for this Book of the prophets is finally closed. Hence the Shepherd of Hermas must be used only for private reading."[1]

If we closely consider what these words say we cannot doubt that the author means that prophetic works (apocalypses) as such do not at all belong to the Canon of the Church. His statement is, however, involved, because as a matter of fact, which he cannot deny, there is question here of three works of prophetic character, two of which he himself allows to stand in the Canon. He thus occupies a position intermediate between two groups in his own Church, one of which would only allow one Apocalypse, while the other would allow three to be read in public. It is noteworthy that, though he does not agree with the former group, their views do not arouse his displeasure ; he only

[1] Lines 71 ff. : "Apocalypses etiam Johannis et Petri tantum recipimus, quam quidam ex nostris legi in ecclesia nolunt. Pastorem vero nuperrime temporibus nostris in urbe Roma Hermas conscripsit sedente cathedra urbis Romæ ecclesiæ Pio episcopo fratre eius, et ideo legi eum quidem oportet, se publicare vero in ecclesia populo neque inter prophetas completo numero, neque inter apostolos in finem temporum potest."

states quite objectively their dissent from himself.[1] On the other hand, he opposes the claim of the other group and rejects it with restrained and yet unmistakably strong feeling.[2] The only conclusion we can draw is that the new Canon when it was formed contained *three* Apocalypses;[3] but that very soon afterwards in Rome itself a protest was raised, with the result that the third Apocalypse was sacrificed to the feelings of a majority while a minority effected the rejection also of the second. The protest was concerned with the question whether Apocalyptic (prophetic) books had any right to be included in the new Canon; and the fact that the Johannine Apocalypse and at first also the Petrine Apocalypse were able to gain a place therein was due, not to their prophetic, but simply to their *Apostolic*, character.

Can we imagine a more striking contrast than that afforded by this later stage and the first

[1] It is the only case of this kind in the whole list. There is no reference to the Petrine apocalypse in Irenæus and Tertullian, unless, in the case of the latter, it is to this apocalypse that we must assign the quotation from an apocryphal work that occurs in *De Resurr.*, 32: "Habes scriptum: 'Et mandabo piscibus maris et eructabunt ossa quæ sunt comesta, et faciam compaginem ad compaginem et os ad os.'" I am sorry to say that I have overlooked this quotation in my article on works quoted by Tertullian; it has been kindly pointed out to me by Mr Tame of Cambridge.

[2] Though not with the unrestrained passion shown by Tertullian in *De Pudicitia.*

[3] Irenæus also, and Tertullian (in his early writings), count Hermas among authoritative works, and thus as belonging to the new Canon.

beginnings of the history of the Canon! Now, at first, *only three* Apocalypses are included, and, finally, all but one are excluded, whilst at the beginning the Apocalyptic and prophetic works—whether Jewish Messianic writings that had not found a place in the Old Testament or new Christian writings—were the *only books* that ranked in authority with the Old Testament. Seeing that the "Word of the Lord" had not yet found definite literary form we may, without exaggeration, say that in those first days the Apocalypses, in idea and, indeed, to a great extent in actual reality, appeared as a second Canon, and accordingly formed the nucleus of a New Testament [1] of definite character which, however, perished at its birth. The Apocalypses of Ezra, Moses, and Enoch are quoted as authoritative in post-Apostolic literature from the Epistle of Jude onward: Hermas quotes no work except a prophecy of Eldad and Modad (*Vis.*, ii. 3, 4); nay, even Paul himself quotes an Apocalypse (Ephes. v. 14), so also the authors of the first and second Epistles of Clement (i. 23; ii. 11). The author of the Didache (ii. 7. 11) forbids any criticism of the utterances of Christian prophets, including naturally written prophecies, indeed he compares such criticism to the sin against the Holy Ghost.

[1] Or of an expansion of the Old Testament. In the treatise *De Cultu Fem.*, Tertullian still pleads for the acceptance of Enoch into the Old Testament of the Church.

This can only mean that the authority of prophecy is absolute and must be accepted unconditionally. The author of the Johannine Apocalypse closes his book with the denunciation of fearful punishments against anyone who dared to alter his prophecy (xxii. 18 f.), claiming thus for his utterances supreme authority. Hermas requires that his little Apocalypse should be read everywhere in the Churches.[1] Justin, in *Dialogue* 81, describes the Millennium first according to Isaiah lxv., then he adds that also " among us " a man named John, in a revelation afforded to him, has prophesied of a kingdom of a thousand years, with which prophecy Justin combines a saying of the Lord. The fact that " among us " the gifts of the prophets still continue (c. 82, etc.) is for Justin a decisive proof that " we " are the people of God. No doubt about it, a Corpus of Christian prophetic writings was well in sight as a new collection of sacred scripture.

Why, then, is it that such a collection has not come down to us as a "New Testament?" Why have the first become last—indeed, not even the last—why have they almost all been thrust into the background?

The answer to this question in its main lines has been already given above: the course of develop-

[1] *Vis.*, 11, 4. The president of the Church is to send it to the Churches in other lands; a certain *Grapte* is to deliver it to the widows and orphans in Rome; Hermas himself will read it to the Roman presbyters.

ment of the inner history of the Church during the years A.D. 150-180 thrust the idea of the "Apostolic" into the foreground as of sovereign authority, and at the same time with ever-increasing emphasis proscribed the idea of the prophetic. The Montanist controversy, indeed, brought this process to its close. Had this controversy not occurred, the process would not only have lasted much longer but it might also have had a somewhat different result. Yet on the other hand we must recognise that this controversy was only an acute symptom of a development whose necessity lay in the very nature of the Church as it consolidated itself. *Every religious community as it grows into a Church based on tradition must proscribe "prophecy" as authoritative.* Prophecy may continue to play its part in the life of the individual and for the edification of smaller groups, it may even preserve an honourable place in the Church itself as an ornament of spiritual value, but it can never be of Canonical authority just because in Churches based on tradition this function *belongs exclusively to tradition itself and to the official body that administers tradition.* These two powers are intimately connected and only perform their function in the absence of a rival authority. In the Churches, however, tradition had necessarily "the Apostolic" as its characteristic. Accordingly, if the development of things demanded that the test of the Apostolic must be applied also to written works, then it necessarily followed that books of prophecy as such must fall out of account unless they could produce some other claim to authority. Their authors had gifts personal in character, but possessed, so to say, no *Missio Canonica.*

According to this fundamental principle almost every prophetic element was eliminated when the new Canon was constructed, about the year A.D. 180, a fact that in itself shows most clearly that the Canon was based on a *selection.* Three Apocalypses were indeed preserved, but the explanation, so far as the Johannine and Petrine Apocalypses are concerned, is very simple. They counted as *apostolic* writings and this saved them.[1] Their apostolic character made them fit to be accepted—and, besides, the Johannine Apocalypse contained seven (hortatory) epistles, as the Muratorian Fragment remarks not without some special reason; we cannot tell whether the Petrine Apocalypse also contained passages of a hortative character. What, however, was it that protected the Shepherd of Hermas when the decision was once made that prophecy was not to be admitted into the new Canon, but was to be confined to the Old Testament? Probably it was at first impossible to do away with

[1] Justin already assigns value to the Apostolic character of the Johannine Apocalypse when he introduces its author, not only as "one of us named John," but also as "one of the apostles of Christ."

the book because its prestige was too high; after all, theory must always come to a compromise with the force of facts! Then again, prophecy occupied only a portion of the book, which otherwise consisted of exhortations of all kinds that afforded no difficulties to the new Canon. And, lastly, it is quite possible that about the year A.D. 180 numbers of people, even in Rome, no longer knew how late the book was, indeed confidently ascribed it to the Hermas greeted by St Paul in the Epistle to the Romans (xvi. 14),[1] thus investing the author with somewhat of an Apostolic character. The fact that the Muratorian Fragment so emphatically states the late date of the book does seem to imply that this was no longer generally known.

But must not the breach with ancient tradition involved in the rejection of prophecy have been felt in the Churches to be revolutionary? This would certainly have been the case if the late Jewish and the Christian Apocalypses had ever been read regularly at public worship; but, then, no such custom can be proved to have existed. It is true, as we have seen, that these works were fairly constantly quoted; but we may be sure that the general knowledge of these works was confined only to isolated utterances from them. Hence the new theory, if it spared the three above-mentioned

[1] This combination is, it is true, first met with in Origen, Comm. in Rom. x. 31.

Apocalypses, could creep in without causing any perceptible breach. Indeed we may say conversely that the new theory could only have arisen because the prevailing practice of public lection had unconsciously prepared the way for it.

It was not until theory began to interfere with this practice that conflicts arose. We hear nothing, indeed, of these in connection with the Petrine Apocalypse; but here we may assume that its authorship by St Peter was called into question at an already early date. Those Roman Christians that, according to the testimony of the Muratorian Fragment, would not have this book read in the Church, in all probability had already denied the Petrine authorship—certainly not on the ground of critical investigations, but, as we may well suppose, because the Apocalypse contained a long discourse of Jesus with the disciples which was not contained in the Gospels, and had a suspicious savour of Gnosticism.[1] What is certain is this, that wherever the book dropped out of use it was regarded as pseudo-Petrine. It disappeared silently and peace-

[1] About the year A.D. 200 numerous works recounting discourses of Jesus with His disciples (especially after the Resurrection) had already come into circulation. The majority of these were heretical and gave offence to the orthodox. This must have caused anxious and sober-minded men, without demanding of them much critical intelligence, to come to the conclusion that *all accounts* concerning our Lord not included in the Gospels were to be rejected, and therefore also the books which contained such accounts. The passage in question in the Petrine Apocalypse must have struck "Canonists" of the straiter sect as very suspicious.

fully, reappearing here and there for a moment before it sank for ever.

The Shepherd of Hermas fought hard against his expulsion. Nothing substantial could be produced in favour of the book except "custom"; and the fact that the book disappeared so slowly shows what a powerful factor custom was in the whole process. The battle against this accepted work started by the author of the Muratorian Fragment on the ground of the new Canonical principle,[1] and continued by Tertullian on Montanist grounds, lasted pretty well through the first half of the third century. It ended, as it could only end, disastrously for the Shepherd, and even Origen's affection for the book could not save it against the new principle. This principle, not the attacks of Tertullian, brought about its destruction; and yet in some Churches (especially the Egyptian and Latin) it still had friends for a long period, and an attempt was even made to preserve the book for the Church by attaching it to the Old Testament.[2]

But even the Johannine Apocalypse during the third century must face the attack of the new principle following upon a preliminary assault by the Alogi. The facts of this conflict and their consequences are so well known that we need not here

[1] There is nothing in what he says that shows that he objected to the contents of the book.

[2] Concerning the most instructive history of the book until far into the Middle Ages, *vide* the Prolegomena to my edition (pp. xliv.–lxxi.).

consider them, and besides they lie outside the limits that have been set to our investigation. Yet they themselves finally confirm the view which we have taken. If objections were raised against the appearance in the Canon of a book so ancient and venerable, how great seems the gulf that separates present and past, how firm and secure the new principle that prophecy as such does not belong to the New Testament! It is true that objection was taken in Alexandria and Cæsarea to the Millennianism and much else that appeared in the book, but the real motive for rejection was that one would have nothing to do with prophetic revelations that altered the impression that one had received from the words of Christ and the Apostles. For this very reason the Apostolic character of the book began to be disputed; for there was no other way to do away with the book. If things had gone as Eusebius really wished, we should not to-day have had the book in the New Testament, but this conscientious accountant could not bring himself to allow his own opinion to override the facts as they stood, which he felt it to be his bounden duty to state and accept. If Athanasius, in his famous Festal Epistle, had accepted the verdict of Dionysius and Eusebius, the book would also have been lost; for at that time the West also was ready to accept or reject all that the great Bishop of Alexandria prescribed. But

Athanasius as a Churchman followed in his list the tradition of his Church, which, in spite of Dionysius, had held fast to the Johannine Apocalypse. Thus the book was finally saved for the New Testament. It was now only a question of time how long a few Oriental Churches would continue to reject it.

The answer to the question set at the head of this paragraph runs thus: The New Testament does not contain several Apocalypses (prophetical books), because, according to the principles which led to its creation at the end of the second century, prophecy as such was absolutely excluded from its sphere; *one* Apocalypse, however, was preserved, because according to these same principles this one as the work of an Apostle could not be absent from the Apostolic Canon.

§ 5. *Was the New Testament created consciously? and how did the Churches arrive at one common New Testament?*

The Dialogue of Justin with Trypho affords the strongest testimony that in the sixth decade of the second century there was no such thing as a New Testament (*vide supra*, p. 16). The Montanist movement gives the same witness (*vide supra*). A movement of its character could never have arisen if a New Testament had then existed. On the other hand, Irenæus, about A.D. 185, is a witness for the new collection of sacred books though not for the closed and definite form which it first acquired in the second period of the Montanist controversy. The Muratorian Fragment, about the year A.D. 200, and Tertullian are the first witnesses that this character had been acquired. The bipartite collection as "Books of the New Covenant" thus came into existence between A.D. 160 and 180, the relatively closed and definite form was acquired between A.D. 180 and 200.[1]

The difference between Irenæus, on the one hand, and the Fragment and Tertullian in their attitude to this question is by no means slight. Speaking strictly, it would be possible for us to say that Irenæus had no New Testament before him; the name does not occur in his works, and though he ascribes the greatest importance to the number four of the Gospels, he is otherwise so unconcerned about the number of the books that, with him, the Gospels seem still to stand apart by themselves. But on closer observation this impression proves false. With Irenæus also the collection has a *definite structure*: Gospels, Acts of the Apostles,

[1] The books of the New Testament are now called "Holy Scripture," and are all quoted with the phrase γέγραπται like the books of the Old Testament; but the influence of earlier custom, according to which the writings of the Old Testament alone counted as Holy Scripture, may still be traced in authors of the third century, with special strength naturally in authors at the beginning of that century.

Pauline Epistles—while the Acts forms the bridge between Gospels and Pauline Epistles legitimising the standing and determining the interpretation of the latter. Moreover, the selection of books is essentially the same in these three earliest authorities. Thus all that is characteristic of the Apostolic-Catholic collection is already given for Irenæus, and in contrast with him the Fragment and Tertullian do not mark a new stage, but a somewhat wider development on the same stage; a development which answered to the development in the general history of the Church during the last two decades of the second century.

1. We are dealing with a period when the Holy Scriptures were still written on rolls. *The fact of a definite structure* ("evangelicæ et apostolicæ litteræ," the latter opening with the Acts of the Apostles) is in itself evidence of the first importance that *the New Testament from a certain point in its development onwards was a conscious creation.*

Critics continue to excuse themselves from boldly facing the question—conscious creation or not. Up to a certain point this reluctance is intelligible and justifiable. In fact, after the four Gospels had once come together in Asia Minor, and after they in their fourfold form had won their way into one Church after another, there is very much in the development of things leading to the foundation of the New Testament that can and ought to be explained from the practice of public reading and other causes, without recourse to the hypothesis of conscious creation. Even the addition to the Gospels of Apostolic Epistles in some form or another is an arrangement that might easily have arisen quite independently and in essentially similar fashion in different Churches. But *the form in which the addition is made under the dominating influence of the Acts of the Apostles* could not have occurred automatically and at the same time in different Churches. I here refer to what has been already written on page 67: *the placing of this book (the Acts) in the growing Canon shows evidence of reflection, of conscious purpose, of a strong hand acting with authority; and by such conscious action the Canon began to take form as Apostolic-Catholic.* It cannot have happened otherwise; for the sense of purpose expressed in the structure cannot have been unconscious. It is not permissible to object that the Acts of the Apostles could not but find its way into the Canon and occupy an important position therein seeing that its author had already found a place there as an evangelist; for the book is not placed next the Lucan Gospel, nor does the name of Luke appear in its title. The latter fact is most important. The compiler does not trouble to give the name of the author, it is of no importance for him; he gives the book the inclusive title,

Πράξεις ἀποστόλων,[1] and seems thereby to suggest that we have here a book that gives the genuine testimony of the Apostles themselves. *Note that the Acts of the Apostles is the only book in the New Testament that does not bear in its title the name of the author!* The book was meant to supply the place of a book which did not exist and could not have existed! This valuation of the book, this new stamp impressed upon it, did not make themselves, they came about because a solid organic Apostolic-Catholic Canon was to be gained thereby.

2. Setting at its highest the measure of uniformity in the different Churches that must have resulted from the relatively small number of early Christian works and from the practice of public reading, we shall still never be able from these causes alone to explain the fact that the Acts of the Apostles, thirteen Pauline Epistles, the Epistles of Jude, etc., *always* and exclusively are found together side by side with the four Gospels. Why

[1] I do not believe that the original title was simply Πράξεις (Tischendorf). Tischendorf here follows his prejudice in favour of *Codex Sinaiticus*, which itself gives Πράξεις Ἀποστόλων in the subscription. The cloud of witnesses from the Fathers proves only that the abbreviated title was in constant use, as was only natural. For a moment the thought might suggest itself that Πράξεις Ἀποστόλων was intended originally to be an inclusive title for the whole second part of the New Testament, and that the Acts had accordingly no separate title; but this hypothesis cannot stand. No manuscript of the New Testament, so far as I know, has the name of Luke in the title of the Acts.

in the world Jude, why two Johannine Epistles, why everywhere throughout the Church thirteen Pauline Epistles? Why are "Apostolici" admitted to the company of the "Apostoli" and yet are limited in the second part of the Canon at first only to Luke and Hermas? Was the Epistle of Jude really in such wide circulation that a whole multitude of Churches was compelled to admit it into the Canon independently of one another? No: apart from the structure the selection of works affords still further assurance that here a conscious will was in final control.

3. Then there is the agreement in the titles of the books as far back as we can trace them, and here the unanimous testimony of the earliest Fathers leads us back to the beginning of the third century. This in itself is a further proof of conscious creation. We have already dealt with the title Πράξεις Ἀποστόλων; but other titles come into consideration, and the unanimity of the testimony in favour of a fixed form of titles is so great that the few exceptions appear insignificant. Again it is probable that the titles, the beginnings, and the endings of some books have been subjected to correction; if so, the fact that these corrections have passed into all manuscripts shows that they must belong to the time of the final formation of the Canon and thus presuppose an authoritative author. I do not, however, propose to discuss this point

because it has not yet been investigated thoroughly and comprehensively.

The *selection* of works, the *structure* of the collection, and the *titles* of the books assure us that in the New Testament, as it stood at the end of the second century, we have before us a compilation that indeed grew up naturally out of the history of the Church of the second century, but only reached its final form through conscious purpose. Why indeed is it that not one of the different, possible Canons mentioned above (pp. 8 ff. and Appendix 2) came into being in some one Church throughout the world? All goes to prove that the new Canon was a conscious production. Where did it arise?

Certainly not in Africa; for the Church there knew, as we learn from Tertullian, that all that it possessed was received from Rome. Just as certainly not in Egypt; for the relations of the Egyptian Churches with the Churches of the Empire were still very slight at the end of the second century. It is therefore most difficult to imagine that a creation of the Egyptian Church could have established itself in the Church throughout the world, while on the other hand, in spite of the slight connection between the Empire and Egypt, developments in the Empire could easily have influenced Egypt. Again, we may exclude all those provincial Churches that consisted at that time of some few scattered communities (a diaspora in the strict sense of the word), which means in the West *all* Churches except Rome. We may neglect also the Churches of Syria in the widest sense of the term, including Antioch. *There remain then only the Churches of the coastal provinces of Asia Minor, of Achaia and Macedonia, and the Church of Rome.* This practically means that *only the Churches of Ephesus, Smyrna* (perhaps also Sardis Pergamum), *Corinth, and Rome stand in question.*

Decision between these ancient and important Churches is difficult because, as we know, they stood in close communication with one another during the second century. Polycarp himself even in extreme old age (at the time of the Roman bishop Anicetus) visited Rome. The Montanist movement was brought before the forum of the Roman Church, and only just escaped recognition by a Roman bishop (Tert., *Adv. Prax.*, 1): in this connection Irenæus addresses a letter to Rome; Dionysius of Corinth writes to Rome and to other Churches; we know of two Epistles from the Roman to the Corinthian Church, and of many other letters from the same Church to Churches of the East. Rome made the difference concerning the keeping of Easter a matter of universal concern, and demanded that it should be settled simply in accordance with Roman custom. Much else might be mentioned that I have collected in my *Lehr-*

buch der Dogmengeschichte, 1.³ S. 480–496, under the title "Katholisch und Römisch." History shows that at that time the geographical centre of Christendom—the region from the West Coast of Asia Minor to Rome—was also the centre of movement in the Church, *and that in this region every care was taken by means of active intercourse both by person and by letter to promote uniformity of development in opposition to centrifugal and heretical influences.* And history also shows that without prejudice to the independence of individual Churches, *the Roman Church possessed an actual primacy in this region.* Under the care and with the leading of this community, and inspired by its exhortation, the Church developed in this central region of Christendom.

So far, therefore, we may say with certainty that the New Testament arose in the central region of the Empire (Ephesus—Rome); that it is a production of the leading Churches of that region—Churches that were determined upon uniformity of development.

If, however, we examine more closely the character of this new creation and then take a comprehensive view of the Muratorian Fragment, the earliest list of works of the New Testament, we may advance a step further.

We cannot determine more exactly than has been already done a particular Church where the fundamental idea of the New Testament was first conceived and realised—the idea, namely, that the Church possessed books that were fundamental documents of a New Covenant in the same sense that the books of the Old Testament were fundamental documents of the Old Covenant. Certain testimony in favour of Asia Minor, both for conception and realisation, is afforded by two Asiatic authors—Melito (about A.D. 180), who knows books of the Old Covenant (therefore also of the New), and an anonymous anti-Montanist (about A.D. 192), who presupposes the existence of a group of writings (not only gospels) as books of the New Covenant,[1] *vide supra*, pp. 36 ff.; while another writer of Asia Minor, Apollonius, only a little later testifies to the unique prestige of Apostolic Epistles. On the other hand, we have certain evidence that books of the New Testament were recognised as such in the Church of Rome at a relatively earlier date, because

[1] The remarkable expression of the anti-Montanist—that he fears to give an impression that in writing he intended to add something *τῷ τῆς τοῦ εὐαγγελίου καινῆς διαθήκης λόγῳ*—is so important, first, because it shows that the Gospel is the ruling factor, and secondly, because it is intelligible only if we suppose that the author pictures the *λόγος τῆς καινῆς διαθήκης* in writings, and that these writings consisted not only of gospels. For if the collection only included gospels, we cannot understand why the author should have feared being suspected of intending to add to the collection by writing his book. Moreover, there is some probability that the author reckoned the Apocalypse of John in the collection, for the words which he uses in this connection (*τῷ λόγῳ τῆς καινῆς διαθήκης μήτε προσθεῖναι μήτε ἀφελεῖν δυνατόν*) are probably not independent of Rev. xxii. 18 f.

the Church of Africa at the time of Tertullian recognised them as such. We do well, therefore, to give no exclusive vote for either Asia Minor or Rome. But the *fundamental idea* of the new collection as " books of the *New Covenant* " does not exhaust its whole nature. Though it is true that, wherever this idea was conceived and realised, it is in the highest degree probable that the Pauline Epistles were also already accepted—for these alone (not the Gospels) testified to the " New " as a " New Covenant "—and that probably the Acts of the Apostles had already received this name, and with the name a certain position of prestige, yet it is the organic *structure* that really makes the definite " New Testament," the closed organic structure linked together by the central position of the Acts of the Apostles—a structure that is for its part closely bound up with the conception of the collection as *Apostolic-Catholic*, or in other words, as a collection of works giving the testimony of the *Apostles themselves*.

It is in the highest degree probable that the responsibility for this structure rests *simply* with the Church of Rome. In the first place our authorities point to Rome. Among these we must also reckon Irenæus. Where he lays stress upon the Apostolic-Catholic standpoint, that is upon the standpoint of a firm chain of tradition, we always see that he stands under the influence of the

Roman Church.[1] Now, it may be due to accident that we do not receive the same impression from writers in Asia Minor. But here we are faced by the following consideration: the three great Apostolic criteria that we find in force at the end of the second century—the *Apostolic* Rule of Faith, the *Apostolic* Canon of Scripture, and the *Apostolic* office of bishops—form a strict unity. They derive from *one* conception, they are mutually dependent upon one another and condition one another, and in their unity are, in my opinion, only historically intelligible *as the reflection and expression of the self-consciousness and ecclesiastical character of the leading Church, the Church "founded by Peter and Paul."* [2] It is not a question of the idea of tradition in general—this idea could have come into force everywhere independently—but of the employment of the idea as the fundamental authority for absolutely everything connected with the Church. Such a practice, always in close connection with the names of Peter and Paul, is specifically Roman. If this is certain,[3] then it is not likely to be without

[1] His other authority, "all the presbyters in Asia who saw John," is *subsidiary*, belongs to Asia Minor, is derived from Papias, and has force only in special cases.

[2] This self-consciousness and this character, already so clearly shown in 1 Clement, were, indeed, thankfully and admiringly recognised by non-Roman Christians of the second and of the beginning of the third centuries. I would recall only Ignatius (Preface to the letter to Rome), Irenæus, and Tertullian.

[3] The great majority of the other Churches—of all we may well say—towards the end of the second century simply did not possess

significance that the first testimony to the *structure* of the new Canon and its strict treatment as *Apostolic-Catholic* comes from Rome. Rather we may declare with great probability that the *moulding of "the collection of books of the New Covenant" into a relatively closed Apostolic-Catholic Canon with its characteristic structure is the work of the Roman Church.*

And this is the impression always left upon us as we return to the Muratorian Fragment. The beginning of this work is most unfortunately lost, and we can therefore only form a conjecture as to the real intention of its author. But three points are quite clear: (1) Though the author speaks with authority [1]—for he feels that all that the Church does or may do in reference to the New Canon is self-evident and requires no defence—yet he does still partly *defend and justify the* acceptance or exclusion of books, and his whole procedure is intelligible only on the supposition that he is addressing himself to *outsiders* who were in great uncertainty as to what should be included in the new collection

a *fixed*, as it were standardised, Rule of Faith such as the Roman Church possessed in her Symbol; this at least is what we learn from investigations that have been made into the history of the Symbol and the Rule of Faith. Such Churches could naturally compile collections of sacred writings, but not *the* New Testament.

[1] For this very reason he must either have been the bishop, or must have written in close understanding with, or under the direction of the bishop. The Fragment derives from Victor or (less probably) from Zephyrinus, or from a Roman cleric writing in accordance with their views.

of sacred writings. To these he proclaims: "This is our custom, and *this must be the custom everywhere in the Church.*"[1] This naïve identification of what the Church of the author does with what is to be done everywhere in the Church is one of the characteristic marks of the work. The attitude is exactly the same as that of Rome in the Paschal controversy.[2] (2) The Apostolic-Catholic standard dominates the Fragment from its opening words concerning the Gospels to the polemic of the conclusion which associates Montanus with Basilides. (3) Just because this standard gives complete security and guarantees in idea a fixed organic form for the Canon, the author has no further interest in determining the number of the books; rather he leaves it open and gives us to understand that, on the basis of the correct standard and in given circumstances, the Church, i.e. *his Church, could in the future accept other books into the Canon.*

Taking all these points into consideration, we can only say: Could the Roman Church—for it is this Church that speaks in the person of the author—so speak and act if it had been *forced to consider other Churches because these also had long possessed*

[1] He only leaves choice free in the case of the Petrine Apocalypse.

[2] "We," *i.e.* the Roman Church, and the "Catholic Church," are interchangeable. The subject in "a nobis" (line 47), "recipimus" (lines 72 and 82), in "ex nostris" (lines 72 f.), is surely the Church to which the author belongs and not an ideal subject; but this "we accept" is equated with "in catholica habentur," etc.

such a New Testament? And conversely, could any Church other than the Roman have given birth to such a work as the Fragment ? No; the Church from which this work proceeds feels herself unfettered and independent in regard to other Churches —only from this point of view is the work intelligible. But this only means that the Roman Church is defining the New Testament for herself in the first place, but therewith also for other Churches. This Church, then, had not received *this* Canon from another Church; she is bound by no tradition in regard to other Churches; she has herself made, and still continues to make, this collection of books; for the Canon is only relatively closed. Nothing in the Muratorian Fragment suggests that the idea of a new collection of sacred writings side by side with the Old Testament was Roman, or that no New Testament in the more general sense of the word previously existed; but the Fragment gives clear testimony that *this* particular Canon is the specific work of the Roman Church, which cherishes, guards, and develops it, and now also delivers it to other Churches as the Apostolic-Catholic Canon to be by them accepted and observed.[1]

First the collection of four Gospels arose in Asia Minor; then in the centre of ecclesiastical

[1] We still trace in the Fragment something of the idea that the Roman Church regarded the Canon as their own, and at the same time as Catholic.

development—in the region bounded by Rome and the west coast of Asia Minor—a larger collection of "Books of the New Covenant" grew up, consisting of the thirteen Pauline Epistles, several Catholic Epistles, the Revelation of John (and other Apocalypses), and lastly the Acts of the Apostles *under this name*—this collection sprang from the common labour and intercourse of the Churches in the face of heresy and Montanism. Finally, the Roman Church gave form to this collection by enforcing throughout the principle of the Apostolic-Catholic, by placing the Acts directly after the Gospels and attaching to it or rather subordinating to it all the other books, and by applying to the Apocalypses the strict test of apostolicity to which all the Apocalypses save one very soon fell victim. This New Testament, clear and intelligible in its structure, and in regard to its content differing little from its immediate forerunners, gradually established itself in the Churches.

Clement of Alexandria does not as yet know this final form of the New Testament; however, he shows that he is influenced by its forerunner.[1] This is not surprising, for Clement was well acquainted with a store of tradition emanating from the Churches of Asia Minor, indeed these traditions were of fundamental importance for him. If we examine his works with a view to constructing the

[1] *Vide* my *Lehrbuch der Dogmengeschichte*, 1.[4] S. 390–394.

collection of sacred writings in use in the Church of Alexandria, we soon discover that this Church possessed the Canon of four Gospels, that it read the Pauline Epistles as sacred and absolutely authoritative works, but that it also recognised a multitude of early Christian writings of various kinds as sacred in various degrees. Among these we find the Acts of the Apostles and, indeed, under this name. But while it is questionable whether any definite collection of sacred writings, standing in any sense on a level with the Old Testament and the Gospels, can be spoken of as existing in the Church of Alexandria—each work, from the Pauline Epistles to the Epistle of Barnabas, stood by itself, each had its own individual significance in the sphere of the holy and authoritative—so it is still more questionable whether the Acts of the Apostles, not infrequently quoted by Clement, belonged to this collection if it existed.[1] It is very possible that the actual position of the Church of Alexandria in regard to the growing New Testament was yet more primitive than it appears in the works of Clement, who by his travels and through his connection with numbers of Churches outside Egypt was well acquainted with their circumstances. If in one of his works he actually commented on 1 Peter, 1 and 2 John, and Jude alone among the

[1] Leipoldt, *Geschichte des Neutestamentlichen Kanons,* 1. S. 200; "Clement does not regard the Acts of the Apostles as canonical."

Catholic Epistles, and when he gives the name Πράξεις Ἀποστόλων to the second work of St Luke, in both cases he is evidently dependent upon the New Testament as it was developing *in the Empire.* The Church of Alexandria seems to have indiscriminately accepted every work that could be possibly regarded as sacred, and as occasion served to have appealed to each as authoritative. Not till the beginning of the third century can this Church have arrived at a more definite selection and structure for its sacred writings. It is surely significant that at this time Origen, the chief of the Catechetical School, visited Rome, and there came into touch with the presbyter Hippolytus, and that since the beginning of the third century general relations between the Church of Alexandria and the Church of the Empire became more intimate than before. When, however, the Church of Alexandria was confronted with the necessity to form for herself a definite New Testament, she found in her midst a greater number of works claiming acceptance than were to be found in the more central Churches of the Empire The Alexandrian Church had long ago taken the Epistle to the Hebrews into her collection of Pauline Epistles and would be reluctant to lose it; again, decision had to be given concerning the Epistle of James, a second Epistle of Peter, and a third Epistle of John, as well as Barnabas, Clement,

Didache, etc. (and Hermas again), all of which presented themselves for acceptance. In accepting and rejecting this Church now openly followed the same principles that were current in Rome, *i.e.* she accepted only what was or seemed to be strictly Apostolic. As a result the New Testament of Alexandria was somewhat more comprehensive than the Roman; so also in other Churches of the East, as the Roman standard gradually came to be accepted and applied to the works that up to this time had been read in each Church, the resulting New Testament in each case disclosed differences sometimes of a plus, sometimes a minus.

The disputes of scholars and Churches concerning these differences, the efforts of Origen, Eusebius, Athanasius, and others in this connection, the final compromise in the second half of the fourth century, the differences still remaining especially in the Churches of the extreme East—all these questions, however necessary it is that they should be discussed, nevertheless involve absolutely no principle of any importance, depending as they do upon the operation of a single insignificant factor. No one now felt empowered to make any change in the compass of the New Testament—the spirit that could soar to the heights of the *recipimus* of the Muratorian Fragment soon died out in the Church. Never since the very beginning of the third century do we hear of even synods dealing boldly with the question of the canonicity of books. All that could be done now was *to count the heads* of Churches and authorities, and the conception of the "Antilegomena" now took form—a conception that was essentially impossible and evasive, and that simply meant a μετάβασις εἰς ἄλλο γένος. Finally, the New Testament, in the form of the more comprehensive Canon of Alexandria, gained the victory also in the West, because it was backed up by the authority of Athanasius and because his manifesto found the Western Churches so situated that they were more disposed to bow before the higher antiquity of the Churches of the East than they had ever been before. The Canon of twenty-seven books, as we still have it to-day, is the Canon of the Alexandrian Church of the third century, but its nucleus is the New Testament as it was created about A.D. 200 in Rome.[1]

After the Roman Church had given form to the new collection of sacred writings and had *in idea* created a closed Canon, this creation functioned so admirably in every Church where it was accepted as a pattern in the course of the third century, that throughout the Churches the New Testament was regarded as if it were as fixed and definite an entity

[1] Indeed, the Homologoumena and the Antilegomena melioris notæ of Eusebius taken together are simply the Alexandrian collection as it was formed at the time of Origen and probably under his influence. Eusebius in his statements concerning the Canon simply follows the lead of Origen.

as the Old Testament, while in truth there was still great lack of uniformity. This is an astounding fact, yet so it happened. For this very reason we are justified in asserting that the Churches arrived at a single New Testament, because in Rome at the end of the second century the new collection of sacred writings attached to the Gospels was organised and crystallised under the influence of a grand and simple conception; because this procedure met with universal acceptance on its own merits backed by the authority of the Roman Church; and because the different and formless collections of the other Churches were so closely related to that of Rome that they could accommodate themselves to the Roman conception without great difficulty and sacrifice.[1]

[1] The best example of a collection of Christian books still *unaffected by the final, namely the Roman, arrangement* is contained in the list called "Catalogus Claromontanus" (Zahn, *Neutestamentliche Kanonsgeschichte*, II. S. 157 ff.): The Four Gospels, the Pauline Epistles, two Epistles of Peter, James, Barnabas, Revelation of John, the Acts of the Apostles, Hermas, Acta Pauli, Apocalypse of Peter. Notice the still subordinate position of the Acts (with Hermas and Acta Pauli) between the two apostolic apocalypses. This position shows that here the influence of the Roman New Testament had not yet made itself felt. The text probably points to Alexandria or to a Church whose collection of sacred books was nearly allied to that of Alexandria.

II

The Consequences of the Creation of the New Testament

From the very moment that the New Testament lay before the Church in the form and in the relatively final arrangement attested by the Muratorian Fragment and Tertullian (*i.e.* the Roman Church) it developed practically *all* the consequences and exercised *all* the influence that as *instrumentum divinum* it could develop and exercise. Its authority was as fully recognised as if only one and the same New Testament stood beside the Old Testament. All the long-drawn developments, starting with the beginning of the third century, that were necessary for the production of a really uniform Canon (of twenty-seven books) had practically no significance for its prestige, which was already perfect, or for its consequent effects, which were immediate. The thorough investigation of these extraordinary effects is a task that ought to have been carried out by historical science, but it has been hitherto neglected. I shall endeavour in the following pages to do justice to the task.[1]

[1] These develop an outline which has been given in my *Lehrbuch der Dogmengeschichte*, I.[4] S. 395 ff.

§ 1. *The New Testament immediately emancipated itself from the conditions of its origin, and claimed to be regarded as simply a gift of the Holy Spirit. It held an independent position side by side with the Rule of Faith; it at once began to influence the development of doctrine, and it became in principle the final court of appeal for the Christian life.*

Any collective body of fundamental sacred documents, as soon as it has taken form, stands at once on its own rights. Whatever the circumstances may have been under which it came into existence, however numerous the forces that contributed to its appearance, however slow and difficult the process of its development—from the moment of its birth all is forgotten. This is true also of the New Testament. As soon as it appeared in its Roman form it was practically regarded as a book that had fallen from Heaven: the Holy Spirit had created it and given it to the Church. Lessing (*vide supra*, p. 19, note 1) was certainly right when he showed that the Rule of Faith is older than the New Testament and had an important part in its creation; but he did not see that, when the New Testament had once come into existence, it immediately renounced its earthly origin and claimed for itself not only a position of equal rank with the Rule of Faith, but in a certain aspect even of superior rank. The daughter at once outgrew the mother, indeed, politely disowned her and set herself in the mother's place. Complicated and energetic measures had then to be taken—the Catholic Churches invented them and set them in motion—to uphold the authority of the mother as against the daughter, and even then all that could be accomplished was either that the mother and daughter should divide the leadership between them in so far as they chose different provinces (the one rather doctrine the other life), or that they should take the lead alternately (*vide infra*).

The Apostolic Tradition of Doctrine and the New Testament.—The curve of movement of doctrine and life in the Church since the beginning of the third century became an ellipse with two foci that at one time approached so closely to one another as to seem one, at another time were quite widely separated. While the Apostolic doctrinal Tradition prevented ecclesiastical Christianity from becoming a religion of the book like Islam, the New Testament prevented the "Apostolic Traditions of the Fathers" from becoming the tyrants of the Church, as in later Judaism. The tension between the Apostolic Tradition and the sacred letter of the New Testament proved in the main beneficial to the development of the Church; extremes threatening from the right and the left were thus warded off. No one has yet written the history of the tension and conflict between the spirit and letter of the Bible on one side and the Rule of Faith on the other before the Reformation. It is true that the New Testament itself in principle and construction was in fact "Apostolic Tradition"; yet not only did it very soon represent an earlier tradition as opposed to a later continually developing tradition, but the independent force of its letter and spirit made itself felt more and more—whether to the advantage or disadvantage of development. No one dared to oppose the authority of the Divine Book; no one any more thought of it as tradition. The learned investigations concerning the origin of particular books conducted by a few theologians, from Origen onwards, had simply "antiquarian" significance. The authors themselves scarcely dreamed of making deductions that would affect the dignity of the Book in question. If they did, the Church either took no notice or marked down such scholars as suspect. The attitude of Tertullian and of his lax opponents in Carthage and Rome, who were in absolute agreement with him in the valuation of the New Testament and in the principles of its use, proves that since the beginning of the third century the New Testament stood as ἀπάτωρ ἀμήτωρ in the Church. No one any longer thought of a time when there was as yet no New Testament; scarcely anyone recollected that the Church had created it. Indeed, solemn eulogies of the New Testament as the book of the Holy Spirit were fairly frequently expressed in terms which implied an *exclusive* relationship between the Holy Spirit and the Book in regard to the Church : all that the Spirit had to say to the Churches He had put into this Book.

The New Testament joins the Rule of Faith in influencing the development of doctrine from the moment that it was fixed in idea. Already in the Adoptianist and Modalistic controversies passages from the New Testament were used as weapons by both sides. In such controversies in the Early Church the influence of the Book was not, however, altogether progressive ; much more often it was a hindrance because of the strenuous opposition that it at first offered to almost every unbiblical formula that Dogmatics declared to be necessary. How difficult it was for "Homoousios" to gain acceptance because it was unbiblical! And, on the other hand, how hard for the orthodox was the fight against a biblical formula if from higher interests they felt compelled to reject it! The battles of orthodoxy against ἔκτισεν,[1] as used of the Sophia (the Logos), and against the formula πρωτότοκος πάσης κτίσεως,[2] tell us something of these things. And yet isolated biblical phrases found their way into Dogmatics; and more than this, Christological passages like that in Philippians ii. have exercised the deepest

[1] (Created.) [2] (Firstborn of all creation.)

influence upon doctrine. Indeed, speaking generally, we may say that though the New Testament did not play the principal part in the battle against heresy, it nevertheless formed the court of final appeal in controversies concerning the Rule of Faith, and never submitted to any tradition, however ancient, that might be opposed to it. Again, whole bodies of doctrine of lesser or greater importance have found their way into Dogmatics simply because they were biblical: the West would never have accepted Augustine's doctrine of Predestination if it had not had such strong support in Romans ix.–xi. This is, indeed, a particularly famous example, and it would be difficult to find another quite like it; but many less important instances could be adduced.

In matters of Christian life the New Testament at once takes a place of central and ultimate authority. Here there was no need to change the ancient formula *πολιτεύεσθαι κατὰ τὸ εὐαγγέλιον*[1] either in letter or spirit. We do not here inquire how far this inviolable principle of Christian life, to which even the Rule of Faith was scarcely allowed to dictate, was actually realised. It is enough to know that in theory no one dared to disturb the principle that a Christian was to live in accordance with the Gospel or *κατὰ τὴν καινὴν διαθήκην*[2] and must be able to appeal to passages

[1] (To live in accordance with the Gospel.)

[2] (In accordance with the New Testament.)

of Scripture as an authority for his manner of life. We only notice how soon this led to the rise of Monasticism, and later to other strictly regulated forms of life. On the other hand, the "Lax" also sought justification for their principles and rules in passages from the New Testament. Here very abundant and interesting material is afforded in Tertullian's treatises. It is the Lax in conflict with a tradition of the Church who ask for the passage of Scripture upon which it is founded. "Ubi scriptum est ne coronemur? . . . expostulant scripturæ patrocinium" (*scil.* for the prohibition against the wearing of garlands).

Lastly, in the first days of the Church reading for private edification was confined to the Psalms, but after the creation of the New Testament the Gospels also gradually came into use—indeed, even the Pauline Epistles. Without the New Testament this would never have happened. What it meant for the deepening of Christian life and thought, that these were nourished on the New Testament and not on the Psalms alone, there is no need to explain.

§ 2. *The New Testament has added to the Revelation in history a second written proclamation of this Revelation, and has given it a position of superior authority.*

In Judaism—not only in the more cultured Judaism of Alexandria—one had long been accustomed to see the Revelation of God to His people in a double form : God has revealed Himself in a long chain of facts, institutions, persons, etc., and He has deposited the content of this Revelation in a book and has thus embodied it permanently for men in written letters. In course of time the book itself became Revelation, indeed *the* Revelation—the double form seemed superfluous—and there arose a kind of *quid pro quo* in that, since the book became Revelation, Revelation itself was regarded as consisting of accounts of events, doctrines, laws, ideas, and so forth. All that happened, happened only that it might be taken up into the book, and that in the book and working from the book it might first effect that for which it was intended. No longer was it a question of Moses, but of *the Law*; no longer of David, but of the *stories* about him, and of the Psalms.

Scarcely was the New Testament created when here also the same idea makes its appearance : the book takes its place beside the facts for which it vouches, indeed it transforms all facts into words, into doctrine. It represents the Revelation of God as a literary revelation, and sometimes it seems as if the revelation in facts of history required this literary revelation at least as a complement, sometimes it seems even to disappear entirely behind the written revelation. The text, " What was written was written for our learning," was understood almost as if it meant, "What *happened* for our learning must be *written*." But the idea is carried still further as we see already in the writings of Origen. God the Creator has brought into existence two great Creations, no more and no less, in which He reveals Himself: the Universe and the Bible (*i.e.* the Old Testament and the New Testament). The Bible is the parallel to the Universe; over both the Holy Spirit brooded and brought them into existence. Both consist of pneumatic, psychic, and material elements. Side by side with the Kosmos stands the Bible. While the one is the outcome of Divine thoughts the other is the Divine system of thought itself. Thus the Christian Revelation acquired a quite different, or rather a "higher" nature; it became a complex of ideas, or, rather, it is proved to be in fact a complex of ideas, because the Revelation is given as a revelation in writing. From this point of view the Christian religion became a religion of a book, namely of the Book of Divine Ideas. Then it necessarily followed that the Revelation in historic fact, including the historic Christ, of which the Book gives the narrative, must fall into the background when compared with the Revelation in writing and must become something symbolic. It is merely "Mythus," while in the Book the "Logos" bears sway. Hence what really matters about Christ is not that as Christ He had an earthly history, but that as the Logos of the written record He reveals eternal truth. But even where things did not go so far, indeed even where speculative theories were rejected, the position adopted in spite of all "Realism" was not so very different. Even here "It is written" expressed the true authoritative Revelation, and the Revelation through historic fact was to be found only in Scripture—nowhere else. All that was revealed must be in accordance with Scripture. Scripture is the fundamental document of doctrine, and scarcely anyone felt an impulse to search for the history that lay behind it. The Revelation upon which Religion and Church were founded is a written thing. When the formula, "The Scriptures and the Lord," still ran, "the Lord" was still something living; when the formula became, "The Scriptures and the Gospel," He had lost something of this attribute of life; when it then became, "The Scriptures and the Gospels," the attribute of life had become already strictly limited in favour of the letter; when finally it came to the formula, "The Scriptures of the Old and New Testament," then the Revelation in history was practically transformed into a revelation in writing. Thus the whole idea of Religion was altered and was fixed in the direction in which, up to this time, it had been developing. Because the Bible of the two Testaments contained an enormous wealth of material of every possible variety, all this belonged to Religion, indeed was Religion. Religion is just as much knowledge concerning what happened on the second day of Creation as it is knowledge of the loving-kindness of God, of the journeys of the Apostle Paul as of the Coming of the Saviour. The content of the teaching and letter of the two Testaments is the content of Religion.

§ 3. *The New Testament definitely protected the Old Testament as a book of the Church, but thrust it into a subordinate position and thus introduced a wholesome complication into the conception of the Canon of Scripture.*

So long as the Church had no New Testament the Old Testament was always in danger so far as its recognition by the Church as an authoritative book was concerned, indeed was in peril of life in the Church. Almost all "heretics" of the second century rejected it, and this of itself shows how difficult it was for many Gentile Christians to sympathise with it. On the other hand, so long as the Old Testament dominated the Church as the sole *litera scripta* the danger was always present that the Christian Religion would not shake itself free of the shell of Judaism, or, in other words, would not be able to give forceful expression to that in itself which transcended Judaism. Once, however, the New Testament was there, both dangers were exorcised with *one* stroke. The ancient conception of "the New Covenant" carried over into a canon of "the books of the New Covenant" had simultaneous effect to the right and the left, and definitely removed the chief difficulties in either direction. Henceforth Jewish Christians became heretics because they had no New Testament—Irenæus already includes them in his catalogue of heretics—and the chief weapon of the heretics in their conflict with the Church and the Old Testament, the weapon which they possessed in their collections of Christian books, was now snatched from their hand.

Though the books of the New Testament were now established as a second Canon side by side with the Old Testament, it was impossible that this arrangement should produce equality of rank in the two Canons. The new Covenant, indeed, would have been quite superfluous if the old Covenant had been perfect; accordingly the new Canon would also have been quite superfluous if the Scriptures of the Old Testament had been sufficient. The new Canon by being attached to the old Canon acquired all the lofty predicates and attributes as well as the whole apparatus of interpretation of the old Bible, and equipped with these extraordinary advantages *at once thrust the old Canon into an inferior position.*[1] In Justin there is as yet no trace of such subordination, for at his time there was no New Testament; but thirty years afterwards in Irenæus it is obvious: "The books of the Old Testament are the books of the *legisdatio in servitutem*, the books of the New Testament are the books of the *legisdatio in libertatem*" (*vide supra*, p. 40). The former books belong to the childhood of mankind. This idea is developed by Tertullian, and comes to complete and most powerful expression in his remarks on the text: "The Law and the Prophets were until John." At last St Paul's fundamental conception could come to its own in the Church, whereas earlier it seemed to lead into the abysses of Gnosticism: the Law is abolished through fulfilment, it is "demutatum et suppletum." Now it could be without danger declared that the Apostles stand on a higher plane than the Prophets of the Old Testament—Novatian has

[1] The circumstances here are similar to those of the relation of the New Testament to the Rule of Faith from the moment that the New Testament came into existence: just as in this case the daughter at once emancipated herself from the mother, stood on her own right, and in many aspects even thrust the mother into a subordinate position (*vide supra* chap. ii. § 1); so also the New Testament at once thrust the Old Testament into a subordinate position after it had received all the latter's predicates of dignity. And yet the unity of the Old Testament and New Testament guaranteed by the same Spirit still abides. Thus Tertullian (*De Orat.*, 22) expressly states: "Nec mirum si apostolus eodem utique spiritu actus, quo cum omnis scriptura divina tum et genesis digesta est, eadem voce usus est"; cf. *Scorp.*, 2: "Lex radix evangeliorum."

expressed this thought most powerfully.[1] The Christian can live from the New Testament alone, but not from the Old Testament alone.

This position, however, involved a multitude of paradoxes; for the Christian must henceforth regard the Old Testament at one and the same time in the following four ways: (1) The Book is the work of the Holy Spirit, and as such of absolute authority; (2) The Book is in every line of it the book of prophecy, and is so far limited in that it does not contain the fulfilment; (3) the Book is the fundamental document of the *legisdatio in servitutem*, and as such is transcended and antiquated by the New Testament; (4) the Book is in every line full of mystic symbols of the truth, and these are present even in those passages which because they contain ceremonial ordinances are abolished. The inevitable result was that the different parts

[1] Novat., *De Trin.*, 29: "Unus ergo et idem spiritus qui in *prophetis et apostolis*, nisi quoniam ibi *ad momentum*, hic *semper*, ceterum ibi non ut semper in illis inesset, hic ut in illis semper maneret, et ibi *mediocriter* distributus, hic *totus effusus*, ibi *parce* datus, hic *large* commodatus." The writers of the Old Testament thus possessed the Holy Spirit "non semper sed ad momentum, mediocriter et parce," while the writers of the New Testament, *like Christ Himself*, possess the Holy Spirit "semper, totum effusum et large commodatum." Here a most important difference is set up, which naturally was not followed out into all its consequences. Here, too, Tertullian is the forerunner, vide *De Exhort.*, 4: "Spiritum quidem dei etiam fideles habent sed non omnes fideles apostoli . . . proprie apostoli spiritum sanctum habent qui *plene* habent in operibus prophetiæ et efficacia virtutum documentisque linguarum, *non ex parte*, quod ceteri" (thus also the Prophets of the Old Testament), cf. *De Pudic.*, 21.

of the book were divided under these points of view though without any recognised principle of division. The story of Creation in six days for instance, as told in Genesis, was always regarded in the Church as a record of absolute and most glorious truth that had been in no sense altered or added to by the New Testament. Much else in the Old Testament remained for the Church on the very highest level of authority. Other parts, however, were subject to a more depreciatory or a doubtful verdict. Slowly, and yet from the very first, the New Testament thrust the Old Testament into the background, and even in the public services of the Church claimed and obtained precedence. The juxtaposition of the Old Testament and New Testament gave rise to investigations concerning the nature of Christianity of which otherwise no one would have thought, and taught a better understanding of the nature of the new religion, as we see at once when we compare the expositions of the early Catholic Fathers with those of the Apologists. How superior are Irenæus and Tertullian to Justin in their knowledge of the nature of Christianity! How far superior is Clement of Alexandria! And even if the advance noticeable in the works of Clement is in great part due to his philosophy, still he also owes much to the four Gospels and, above all, to the Pauline Epistles. Lastly, the fact that the Canon of Scripture contained in the Old Testament something that was "relative" was of great importance. The numbing influence of Biblicism, otherwise inevitable, was thus warded off. That the Christian religion did not become a religion of "the book" in the full sense of the word is due, next to the fact that the "Rule of Faith" had authority side by side with the Bible, to the fact that in the Bible itself there was this tension between the Old Testament and New Testament. The inconsistency and inconvenience of having in the sacred Oracles of God elements of graduated, indeed sometimes antiquated, value were undoubtedly fraught with good. The New Testament has secured the continuance of the Old Testament in the Church, and at the same time has guarded against the stunting effect of its Judaism, just because the Old Testament was thrust into an inferior position by the New Testament. Moreover, the way to the *historical* treatment of the two Testaments was thus left open for future ages. Tentative beginnings of such treatment already manifest themselves in Irenæus and Clement, who here follow St Paul. But they would not have been able to follow St Paul if collections of epistles of the Apostle had not been already in existence, equipped with an authority to which they could appeal.

§ 4. *The New Testament has preserved for us the most valuable portion of primitive Christian literature; yet at the same time it delivered the rest of the earliest works to oblivion, and has limited the transmission of later works.*

The first clause of the heading of this paragraph requires no proof. It is by no means certain that the Pauline Epistles would have been handed down to us if as a collection they had not been canonised. The author of the Second Epistle of Peter and Irenæus complain of the difficulties which they contain, indeed they presented a thousand stumbling-blocks to the orthodox teacher, and were exploited in a most irritating way by heretics in opposition to the doctrine of the Church.[1] Nor was it otherwise with the Johannine Apocalypse: the Canon alone has preserved it from oblivion. Both in form and content it presented most troublesome stumbling-blocks to the Church, more troublesome indeed as time went on. And further, can we be sure that the Acts of the Apostles, from the historical point of view the most valuable work of primitive times—to say nothing of works so small as the Catholic Epistles—would have come down to us if it had not found its way into the new

[1] How troublesome were such expressions as, "The god of this world," or the doctrines of Predestination and of the Divine hardening of the heart, or the teaching that the Law multiplied transgressions, etc.!

Canon? Even in the third century the Christology of this book would have given grave offence if the fact that the book was Canonical had not barred for ever the question whether it was everywhere orthodox. And what of the Gospels? If it had been possible in the third and fourth centuries to cite them before the Court of the Church, how sadly they would have fared! Even against the Gospel of St John an orthodox judge would have been compelled to admit a heavy catalogue of offences! The Canon, however, settled these questions once and for all. There can be no doubt here: we have to thank the New Testament that we possess these works, that we have in our hands an important and trustworthy account of the beginnings of the Christian religion. We need only reflect for a moment what our knowledge of the beginnings of Christianity would have been if the Church History of Eusebius had been our sole authority—leaving out of account what this work owes to the New Testament—in order to see clearly what it means that twenty-seven early Christian writings have been preserved for us because they were bound together in the New Testament.[1]

[1] We not infrequently hear high praise given to the historical "tact" with which the books of the New Testament were selected; "tact," however, played no part here. If we consider in the first place the Roman Canon at the end of the second century, "tact" resolves itself into a succession of historical necessities which originated in the practice of public lection and in a growing acceptance of the Apostolic-Catholic principle. These explain the acceptance

But, on the other hand, with the creation of the New Testament begins the death struggle of that portion of Early Christian literature that had not found acceptance in the Canon. I have dealt with the story at length in the Introduction to the first volume of my *Altchristliche Lit.-Geschichte.*[1] It is not a question of the loss of *early heretical* works—the New Testament scarcely had anything to do with this—but of the loss of *early orthodox* works. Such works, which were originally to be found in the more extensive sacred collections of some provincial Churches, especially the Alexandrian, must now yield to the stern Roman Law of the Canon, and were for the most part separated away and delivered to death under the reproach that they were interlopers, that their very existence

of the four Gospels, of the collection of Pauline Epistles, and, finally, of the Acts of the Apostles. The latter book was accepted not through the exercise of historical "tact," but because the situation produced an instinctive demand for a book of all the Apostles. Even the reception of four Gospels was determined certainly not by historical "tact," but most probably could not have been avoided if it were wished to keep together the orthodox Christians of Asia. The Gospels of the Hebrews and of the Egyptians were in favour, we may definitely assume, with relatively small and isolated circles, and the Gospel of Peter was too late in its appearance. Moreover the expansion of the Canon to twenty-seven works, to be regretted by no one (what about 2 Peter ?), was not due to the historical "tact" of the Church, but to the apostolic names of the authors of the added books. And it was because Hermas, 1 and 2 Clement, Barnabas, etc., could not satisfy the demand for apostolic origin that they were at last barred from the New Testament.

[1] Bd. 1, p. xxi. ff. *Cf.* also the history of the transmission of 1 and 2 Clement, Barnabas, Hermas, in my edition of these works.

was a piece of insolence, that they were forgeries, and so forth. As a matter of fact they looked like rivals of the works of the New Testament, and must be treated accordingly. There was no middle course; either they must be accepted, or they must be done away with under more or less serious charges. But here an ironical Nemesis intervened, and has preserved for us some early forms of the New Testament (or copies of such forms) in which some portions of this literature still stand! Thus the New Testament, whose intention was to slay these works, was compelled to preserve some of them.[1] It is in this way that the first and second Epistles of Clement, the Epistle of Barnabas, Hermas, lastly also the Didache, have come down to us, as well as large portions of the Apocalypse of Peter, of the Acts of Paul, and of the Diatessaron of Tatian. At first, even after the rejection of the books, their treatment in the Churches was more indulgent than it afterwards became. The Muratorian Fragment, which rejects the Shepherd of Hermas, still favours the private reading of the book, and even as late as the fourth century "Antilegomena" are recommended by Athanasius for the instruction of catechumens. But even this connivance soon came to an end.

This destructive influence of the New Testament

[1] I have no doubt that the Constantinopolitan manuscript of the Didache ultimately proceeds from a manuscript of the Bible.

had, however, yet wider scope. "Quid necesse est in manu sumere quod ecclesia non recipit," says Jerome, and the Spanish bishops upheld the same view against Priscillian, with his noteworthy preference for Apocrypha. "Omne quod dicitur in libris canonicis," they declared, "quæritur et *plus legisse peccare est.*" Here stands the very principle of Biblicism which, strictly applied, must have destroyed *all* Christian literature and must have cut off all hope of a future resurrection. The New Testament might have become a Koran! What need was there of other books? Either they contained what was in the New Testament, then they were superfluous; or they contained other things, then they were dangerous. The Roman Church, from the time of Damasus onwards, proceeded far along this road. Only read the Decretum Gelasianum! If things had gone in accordance with this decree, what would have been left for us of the literature of the first three centuries? Standing upon the New Testament it condemns practically everything else. Now it is true that the ordinances of this decree could assert their authority only to a limited extent, and that they were counteracted by other influences connected with the New Testament, of which we shall speak in the following paragraph; yet there can be no doubt that in the decree a judgment is expressed that tended to cramp Christian literary activity and to hinder *the transmission of earlier works. The great lack of books* always noticeable in the Early *Church of Rome,* and the literary unproductiveness of the Roman clergy, must be understood and judged from this point of view.

But while pointing out the fact that the New Testament hindered the transmission of non-canonical Christian literature and continued to limit its production, we do not mean to assert that this was in every aspect disadvantageous. The hindrance was rather, especially in one special direction, truly happy in its consequences; for, as early as the second century, an inferior literature began to spring up in the Church, increasing in luxuriance from century to century—a literature that was greedily read and that threatened to stifle all feeling for historical truth and for simplicity and purity in religion—that confused mass of apocryphal acts of Apostles, fabricated stories of martyrs and ascetics, ghastly Apocalypses, inventions concerning the Childhood of Jesus, and the like. Side by side with the Canonical Scriptures this literature is represented in every quarter and in every language of the Church by works all essentially similar in character though varying somewhat according to the taste of the time. Much of this literature was really Apocryphal, *i.e.* it carried on a kind of underground existence, appearing again and again at the surface and exercising, in ever increasing degree, a most remarkable influence upon cultus and religious life. Not only many customs, but even Sacraments and Sacramental rites of the Catholic Church took their form under this influence. *If the New Testament had not been in existence, the Church would have fallen a complete victim to this literature.*[1] Standing, however, upon the New Testament, the Church repressed the Apocrypha and repeatedly forbade the reading of these books. The Rule of Faith was useless here; armed only with this, the Church would have been defenceless in this situation. But the New Testament safeguarded the Church, because it stood on a height to which these Apocrypha could no longer attain. It held these books down under its strong hand, and prevented their tendencies from coming to full development; it barred the way to the Ambo and Altar, and saved the true portrait of Jesus from complete obliteration. If the New Testament had not occupied since the beginning of the third century the position of central authority in the Church, all Churches would have probably become Ethiopian. There is no need of proof here; for there was absolutely no other authority in the Church except the New Testament that could have warded off the throttling hand of the Apocrypha.

[1] This happened to the Monophysite Churches in spite of the New Testament.

§ 5. *Though the New Testament brought to an end the production of authoritative Christian writings, yet it cleared the way for theological and also for ordinary Christian literary activity.*

Whatever authorities might arise in the Church and whatever books might be written after the creation of the New Testament, they could no longer attain to the absolute prestige possessed by the New Testament.[1] They could be "inspired," but they could not longer become "canonical" in the sense of the New Testament.[2] Taken all in all, this was a blessing. The literature of enthusiasm now either ceased or was forced to confine itself within the narrow bounds which now restricted its significance and therefore its influence. Naturally the early belief that every Christian who wrote with a view to edification did this by inspiration of the Holy Spirit, now faded away. It was a belief that had placed the primitive Church in positions of terrible perplexity and afflicted conscientious authors with qualms of anxiety as to whether they were not guilty of presumption in taking up the pen. Clement of Alexandria still shows this anxiety—so also the anti-Montanist of Euseb., *H.E.*, v. 16, 3 (*vide supra*, p. 37). But

[1] We here do not take account of the development of General Councils and of the Papacy.

[2] Not even the works of Cyprian.

now this anxiety was no longer felt, and the way was free for the development of theological and ordinary Christian literature. Churchmen could at last with free conscience do what heretics had long done—compose theological treatises, write commentaries, publish edifying stories, and so forth. If only they made up their minds to be "true to Scripture," and in all due humility to serve the Church, no objection could be taken to their work. Indeed the New Testament itself created a demand for the most important part of this literature, for every sacred document must be explained and must be defended against false interpretations. Hence this form of literary activity became at once a matter of duty, and the corresponding literary productions as "Science of the New Testament," if we may use the expression, thus as "Bible-Science" at once acquired the freedom of the Church. Thus the New Testament, which as we saw in § 4 exercised in one particular direction a strongly cramping influence upon literature, in another direction promoted it and opened a new path for it. And what was there that did not come within the scope of the science of the Bible! If the Bible was a cosmos, like the universe, it needed for its interpretation simply every form of Science! And so since the beginning of the third century grew up, attached to the New Testament, the multiform Science of the Church, which began to compete with the Science of the Gnostics and drove it out of the field. In company with this there appeared a multitude of ecclesiastical treatises dealing with every possible problem of the Christian life. There was also a development of practical religious literature that raised no claim to stand on a level with the New Testament, but rather extracted from the New Testament the edifying teaching that it offered to the Churches. Lastly, the way was now opened even for a light literature with religious colouring; for the idea of literature was no longer objectionable, and one could make use of it in every direction so long as one paid due homage to the Holy Scriptures. All this had been brought about by the creation of the New Testament!

§ 6. *The New Testament obscured the true origin and the historical significance of the works which it contained, but on the other hand, by impelling men to study them, it brought into existence certain conditions favourable to the critical treatment and correct interpretation of these works.*

There is no need of many words to show how far the New Testament at first obscured the true origin and significance of the works which it contained. Within a sacred fundamental document everything must be regarded as equal in value, character, and significance. Canonising works like whitewash; it hides the original colours and obliterates all the contours. The Synoptics must be interpreted according to St John, the Pauline Epistles according to Acts: all stand on *one* plane.[1] But much more than this: each separate passage must contain the highest, the best, the most infallible that can be imagined in this connection, and everything must always sound in unison. The New Testament is the ἓν καὶ πᾶν, and in reference to all theological questions it is sufficient, consistent, and clear. Under such presuppositions, how could the actual intention, or indeed anything of the original significance of the works, make themselves felt? Already in Tertullian—both in his own use of the New Testament as well as in that of his Lax opponents—we may observe all the fatal consequences for history of the canonisation of the books of the New Testament. Only one example! In St Matthew's Gospel Magi make their appearance and no fault seems to be found with them as such. Therefore concluded some Lax Churchmen, even a Christian might have dealings

[1] The unanimity of all the Apostles is an axiom for Tertullian in his controversy with Marcion. In several places he brings it to clear expression, e.g. *De Pudic.*, 19: "Totius sacramenti interest nihil credere ab Joanne concessum quod a Paulo sit denegatum. Hanc equalitatem spiritus sancti qui observaverit, ab ipso deducetur in sensum eius."

with magic. Tertullian could not with confidence reject this conclusion ; for it was held as an axiom that what Holy Scripture does not blame it allows.[1] He therefore resorts to a way of escape—the Gospel states that the Magi returned home *by another way* ; the other way, however, means that the Magi gave up their magic.[2] *The inspired canonical document itself imposes the empirical and allegorical method of interpretation.* Whether this method is employed "according to principles" and "scientifically," or empirically case by case, makes no difference in the result : the original sense is always lost and the exegete no longer even seeks for it, but broods over the allegorical sense, *i.e.* over the thoughts which he has to *read into* the text.

But, on the other hand, the instinct for simple truth is not so easily destroyed, and the New Testament to a certain extent came also to its help. The mere fact that works all of *one* historical period were here compiled together was an advantage. The careful observer could not but perceive that in many places they did actually complete and interpret one another. If he had had to deal with each particular book in isolation, how much more perplexed he would have been and how much

[1] Tertullian, it is true, would like to contest the validity of this axiom, but he does not feel that he is on sure ground in doing so.

[2] *De Idol.*, 9.

less vivid must have been the impression he would have received from it! Now, however, once the New Testament had been created, there arose a real science of exegesis, not only the exegesis of allegory which sublimated and thus neutralised the content of the works, but an exegesis which concerned itself, if only in a limited degree, with their historical origin and their literal sense. Even the difficulties presented by the New Testament as a compilation of separate books rendered such investigations quite unavoidable for thoughtful Christians. If, for instance, there had been only *one* Canonical Gospel, Science would have simply capitulated to it; it would have been pure insolence for the human intellect to act otherwise; but the four Gospels in countless passages summoned the intellect to a work of reconciliation. Naturally recourse was had to harmonising; but even in harmonising there lies a true critical element, and in the very process of harmonising it can assert itself. Think only of the critical efforts of Julius Africanus, of Origen, and others who lived soon after the creation of the New Testament; one cannot but see that these efforts would never have been made if the works that they studied had not stood in a *collection*. Again, in the same collection the Pauline Epistles and the Acts of the Apostles stood face to face. This fact also challenged investigation, and every investigation educates the critical sense and inspires it to further efforts! There is, moreover, the fact that the method of Origen, the alchemist of theology, demanded the investigation of the literal as well as the spiritual sense, and that he showed a truly scientific interest in the discovery of the genuine text. Interest in the literal sense and the genuine text of early Christian works would scarcely have arisen if these works had not been combined in the New Testament and regarded as canonical. *Accordingly the creation of the New Testament of itself called into being a critical and historical treatment of the canonical books.*

§ 7. *The New Testament checked the imaginative creation of events in the scheme of Salvation, whether freely or according to existing models; but it called forth or at least encouraged the intellectual creation of facts in the sphere of Theology, and of a Theological Mythology.*

Among historians no doubt can exist that the Gospel history contains a very large number of events that are unhistorical, more especially in the accounts of the Infancy and Resurrection (but also in other passages), and there is also no doubt that legends, whether connected with the scheme of Salvation or called forth by some other motive, continued to increase in number. Now we have already in § 4 called attention to one important fact about the New Testament, namely, that by its very existence as an authoritative document it severely restricted the growth of legend as this continued in the Apocryphal writings. We must now add that the New Testament in every direction, and to an extraordinary degree, exercised a *moderating and restraining influence.* When it was once created, leading Christians in the different Churches no longer allowed themselves to invent facts in connection with the scheme of Salvation, such as were invented in times past, whether by free imagination or according to existing models (the Descent into Hell, the Ascension, etc.). Rather it was felt that everything in the nature of fact had been already given in the New Testament, and that its narratives, even though they might be doctrinal in character, admitted of no additions of the nature of fact. A certain spirit of religious restraint took possession of a great part of the faithful—a spirit that, indeed, always makes its appearance where a sacred book comes into the foreground, for the book itself restrains even the most undisciplined imagination.

But now mischief appeared from another quarter. The book stood as a sacred Canon. The interpreter of the book was guided by principles which affirmed absolute possibility of combination of passages from any part of the book, absolute

10

perfection, absolute unanimity of the writers, the validity of allegorical interpretation, and so forth. Such principles would necessarily lead the interpreter to the construction of new facts generally in the form of a mythology of ideas in which the ancient mythology lived on, only in a higher sphere. What was there that one did not now learn about God, His Nature, His Trinity in Unity, His properties, His operation, etc., if one only made proper combinations! What was there that one was not able to say about Christ as Logos—before Creation, in Creation, after Creation up to His earthly manifestation, and again after His death! What was there that could not be culled from the New Testament concerning His two natures, and how much richer became even His earthly life if only the interpreter was skilful! Even a developed doctrine of the Holy Spirit could be constructed by exegesis! It is true that exegesis was always open to suggestions from the developing science of Dogmatics, and that it was forced to do much that it would never have done except at the bidding of Dogmatics; yet, apart from this, the New Testament itself, if its claims were accepted, necessitated this almost trivial and even revolting multiplication of mythological details without any feeling for reality or sense of history. Thus, though it is true that the New Testament has the merit of checking, indeed of partly stopping, the creation of new, authoritative, realistic legends, and of exercising a restraining influence upon the legends that already existed, yet, on the other hand, it partly summoned the intellect to, and partly encouraged it in, the creation of facts in the sphere of theology and of a theological mythology.

§ 8. *The New Testament helped to demark a special period of Christian Revelation, and so in a certain sense to give Christians of later times an inferior status; yet it has kept alive the knowledge of the ideals and claims of Primitive Christianity.*

The delimitation of a period of fundamental Christian Revelation is in the first place to be explained as a reaction against Montanism, and the creation of the New Testament is in part the consequence of this conception (*vide supra*, pp. 35 f.). But as soon as the New Testament was created it became itself the strongest barrier in the line of division. The present time now appeared as a much inferior thing when compared with the time of Revelation, and accordingly the Christians of the present appeared inferior to the "heroes" of that time. This line of division it is true was not drawn in complete sharpness until the arrival of Protestantism — Catholicism possessed and still possesses points of view that help to attenuate it[1]—yet even to the Catholics of the third century the primitive times appeared as an heroic age, with which they scarcely dared to compare their own times (*cf.* what Origen says on this point). That time was still the epoch of "Spiritual Power," of miracle, and of pneumatic gifts; the present possessed such power only in smallest measure. There was also something comforting in this belief; for now one need not apply to oneself and to one's own time the high standard that those early Christians satisfied; at most it would still apply only and in part to the Clergy.[2] That the primitive epoch was unique was evident also from the fact that books like those of the New Testament could no longer be written.[3] If communion with God might only be reached with the help of a book, and if Divine direction could only be received by means of the same, it followed that the Church of the present was inferior to the Church of the past; there had been a *classical* time, but it had passed away; it had been brought to an end by the Book.

[1] One need think not only of monasticism but also of the saints of all ages and the Evangelical Counsels.

[2] Note how Tertullian as a Montanist scoffs at this attitude, *De Monog.*, 12: "Cum extollimur et inflamur adversus clerum tunc unum omnes sumus, tunc omnes sacerdotes, quia sacerdotes nos deo et patri fecit. Cum ad peraequationem disciplinae sacerdotalis provocamur, deponimus infulas et impares sumus."

[3] Even a Tertullian challenges Marcion: "Exhibeat Marcion dei sui dona, aliquos prophetas . . . edat aliquem psalmum, aliquem visionem, aliquam orationem, dumtaxat spiritualem, in ecstasi, *i.e.* amentia si qua linguae interpretio accessit," etc. (*Adv. Marc.*, v. 8).

But, on the other hand, if the Book had not been created, then it is most probable that even the memory of the forces and ideals that bore sway in Gospel history and throughout the Apostolic epoch would have vanished. Of what enormous importance it was that in the present the authentic records of that past time were still read again and again! How mighty has been the influence of the reading of the Gospels upon the character and course of Church history! Think of the part that has been played by the story of the Rich Young Man or the Sermon on the Mount, and of what it meant for the Church—that Augustine, at the critical moment, opened the Epistle to the Romans! Though no one any longer dared to set himself on the level of the New Testament, still this Book, just because as an authoritative collection it was more or less accessible to all, was a continuous source of power that raised the weak men of the present to heights of perfection. What would have happened if, with the Old Testament, we had received the Didache or the Apostolic Canons and Constitutions as a second Canon, instead of the New Testament? Thus here also the New Testament worked in two contrary directions: it lowered and also raised the tone! It has blunted the conscience of many—no one can attain to the height of the New Testament, nor need one—and it has also acted as a spur to the conscience. It has guarded Christianity from the rank growth of emotionalism, but it certainly has also repressed many a primitive and vital impulse. How many Christians of note with original Christian experience have as "Bible-believers" entangled themselves in the Book, have suffered themselves to be disturbed, hindered, directed by texts of the Bible, and in consequence have not brought their character and innate gift to perfect development, and have lost their freedom! What mischief has been wrought by the Revelation of John just because it stood in the New Testament! What terrible perplexities of conscience have been brought about by certain sayings of St Paul just because they belonged to the Canon! And yet, on the other hand, how unspeakable the blessing that has flowed from passages of the Bible which, just because they were canonical, filled men's hearts with confidence steadfast as a rock!

§ 9. *The New Testament promoted and completed the fatal identification of the Word of the Lord and the Teaching of the Apostles; but, because it raised Pauline Christianity to a place of highest honour, it has introduced into the history of the Church a ferment rich in blessing.*

In the course of the second century the Word of the Lord and the teaching of the Apostles became more and more intimately identified with one another (*vide supra*, p. 48 : ἡμεῖς καὶ Πέτρον καὶ τοὺς ἄλλους ἀποστόλους ἀποδεχόμεθα ὡς Χριστόν) [1]; to this process the New Testament set its seal. The consequences of this identification, not only for Christian Dogmatics but also for the Christian life, were immeasurable and as a rule unfavourable. Not only was religion thereby transformed into the *doctrine* of the Apostles, but also one was now forced to give to particular and very subjective utterances and injunctions of St Paul a weight, which even that exacting Apostle would never have desired. Though the sayings of the Gospel still preserved their special significance for the conduct of life, they yet acquired a powerful rival in the injunctions of St Paul. What, however, was more serious was that, because of this identification, Christology not only took its place beside Christ but even threatened to push Him aside—indeed actually did so. The simplest consideration of the picture of Jesus as given in the Gospel suffered from the troubling and obscuring influence of this "doctrine of the New Testament." It is not possible nor is it necessary to dilate upon this point; but let it be remembered that St Paul also had in the end to suffer from this

[1] How significant it is that already in the time of Hadrian the heathen author Phlegon could so misunderstand as to confound Peter and Christ in narratives (*vide* Orig., *c. Cels.*, II. 14)! This mistake could never have been made if Christians had not placed Peter so near to Christ.

identification. For after a way had been opened for a more liberal conception of the New Testament and a more unbiassed estimate of historical events and persons, critics still made demands of this man as a person and an author that they made of no other man. This disposition was only a lasting relic of the old conception ; men's minds were ever haunted by the spectre of the Canon. Either they laid violent hands on the man, robbed him of a part of his soul, and modelled him into a figure of strictly logical consistency—for was he not once Paul of the New Testament ? and even if he is that no longer, still he must be a type—or they were disgusted with him, heaped upon him complaints and reproaches which they would never have made if they had not received him out of the New Testament. Still this martyrdom of the Apostle continues; still critics who are elsewhere impartial will not allow him a man's right to be more *and also less* than his own type and his own ideal.

Nevertheless, this identification of the Word of the Lord and Pauline doctrine has been full of blessing in an important direction. The New Testament, through the acceptance of the Pauline Epistles, has established as a standard the loftiest expression of the consciousness of Salvation and of the religion of Faith. Accordingly the New Testament, once it was created, exercised an extraordinarily important influence upon the development in the Church of the second century, by which the Christian religion was on the point of being definitely established as the *Religion of the New Law.* If things had gone further in the Church simply on the lines marked out for us in Barnabas, Hermas, 2 Clement, and the apologists, all Christianity would have been gradually reduced within the meagre conception of a new, even though more spiritual, legalism, and at last Marcionites and Gnostics would have been the only people that definitely placed the idea of Salvation in the centre of their religion. That this did not happen is due in great measure to the New Testament—that is, to the fact that the Pauline Epistles were in the Canon, though not, it is true, to that fact alone. Only consider how important the Pauline Epistles were for the thought and teaching of Irenæus, how impossible for him such conceptions apart from these epistles as an absolute authority! Only think what decisive influence the Pauline doctrine of justification exercised in the controversy between Calixtus and the Rigorists concerning penance already at the beginning of the third century! Remember only how the idea of Salvation "by Faith alone" slowly gained ground in the religious thought of the Church until, in the line of Jovinian and others, it at last came to full development in (Ambrose and) Augustine![1] All this was accomplished by Paul *because he stood in the New Testament.* And now further remember what reformations in the course of the history of the Church have been brought about by Paul accepted in the Canon, and what a ferment his teaching has ever been! Up to and beyond the time of the Jansenists Paul is still always at work in the Catholic Church—to say nothing of the German Reformation—and forcibly reminds her what Religion at its best should be and is, and what Faith and Sonship mean. The Apostle would have been shut off from all these activities if he had not come into the New Testament. Whether they outweigh the disadvantages that have resulted from the identification of the "Word of the Lord" and the "Teaching of the Apostles," who can tell?

§ 10. *In the New Testament the Catholic Church forged for herself a new weapon with which to ward off all heresy as unchristian; but she has also found in it a court of control before which she has appeared ever increasingly in default.*

The New Testament was not created as a weapon in the conflict against heresy; there were many

[1] *Cf.* my article "Geschichte der Lehre von der Seligkeit allein durch den Glauben in der alten Kirche" (*Zeitsch. f. Theol. u. Kirche*, i. 1891, S. 82–178).

things in it that rendered it a very inconvenient weapon in this conflict,[1] and that forced Tertullian to give the rather questionable and, indeed, useless warning not to engage in exegetical controversies with heretics, seeing that victory in such conflicts was uncertain or even improbable. Yet, however that might be, the New Testament, when once it was in existence, did form an excellent means of defence and offence against heresy. In the first place one might now simply adopt the standpoint: he who does not accept Scripture is *eo ipso* no Christian—there was thus no need of further discussion. Or just as one denied to the Jews their property in the Old Testament, so now, by declaring that the New Testament belonged to the Church by Divine grant, one might chase heretics away from this Book and proclaim it to be abominable insolence, theft, and robbery that they should even

[1] This inconvenience was so keenly felt by Tertullian, that he even felt compelled to invent a theory by which it might be removed. Seeing that heresies "must arise," the Old Testament and New Testament contain passages that could give rise to heresy; see especially *De Resurr.*, 63: "Quia hæreses esse oportuerat, ut probabiles quique manifestentur, hæ autem sine aliquibus occasionibus scripturarum audere non poterant, idcirco pristina instrumenta quasdam materias illis videntur subministrasse, et ipsas quidem iisdem litteris revincibiles." It is true that he does not feel comfortable about this theory if it is to stand alone; therefore as a Montanist he proceeds: "Sed quoniam nec dissimulare spiritum sanctum oportebat quominus et huiusmodi eloquiis superinundaret quæ multis hæreticorum versutiis semina subspargerent, immo et veteres illorum cespites vellerent, *idcirco iam omnes retro ambiguitates et quas volunt parabolas aperta atque perspicua totius sacramenti prædicatione discussit* per novam prophetiam de paracleto inundantem."

venture a claim to the books contained in the New Testament. Such is already Tertullian's procedure (*De Præsc.*, 37); "Non Christiani nullum ius capiunt Christianarum litterarum, ad quos merito dicendum est: qui estis? quando et unde venitis? quid in meo agitis, non mei? quo denique, Marcion, iure silvam meam cædis? qua licentia, Valentine, fontes meos transvertis? qua potestate, Apelles, limites meos commoves? mea est possessio, quid hic, ceteri, ad voluntatem vestram seminatis et pascitis? mea est possessio, olim (?) possideo, prior possideo . . . ego sum hæres apostolorum!" The Church regarded the New Testament as her own peculiar possession divinely granted; she named herself the Church of the New Covenant with the same title as the book; in conflict, if it seemed fitting, she retired simply into this fortress; and firmly established herself, and gradually her adversaries also, in the conviction that Church and New Testament formed an exclusive unity, so that none but the Church had a right to the works contained in the Canon.

But in the New Testament the Church had created a possession that from her point of view was of very questionable advantage. Her Rule of Faith could be stretched, and was capable of development. The Church managed with it not so badly; when necessary, she treated it as invariable; where need became imperative, she modified and developed it, and could always draw a veil over these developments, such as they were. But it stood otherwise with the New Testament; *littera manet!* Even here, it is true, much that was desirable could be accomplished by manipulation, namely, by "interpretation"; but the letter full often set impassable bounds to such operations. The existence of a written fundamental document that could be held up as a mirror before the Church must have become as time went on more and more inconvenient and dangerous. And it was so employed—by no means only by heretics, but, at first rarely and reluctantly, then more and more frequently, by faithful members of the Church. A beginning was already made by Origen, who earnestly and conscientiously measures the Church by the standard of the New Testament; and numbers of preachers in the Ancient Church followed his example. They themselves had no thought of leaving the Church because on the ground of the New Testament they had found so much fault with her; but even in their times the official Church had begun to consider whether she could tolerate members that with a certain recklessness held up the mirror before her, and she ended by deciding that she could not. Her judgment to-day is still the same. Yet since the time of the Waldensians and the Franciscans, what assaults have been made upon the Church from the base of the New Testament! What foes have drawn their weapons from this armoury and have forced the Church to fight hard for life! It is because the Church carried the New Testament with herself and before herself that reformations, that the Reformation, became possible; and the Reformed Church at least, because she must recognise this New Testament, must accept all that is drawn from this Book for her correction. Thus this collection of sacred writings has proved a great arsenal and a court of appeal for critics of the Church! When it was created, who could have suspected that this would be? The old proverb, "Habent sua fata libelli," has here received most remarkable confirmation.

§ 11. *The New Testament has hindered the natural impulse to give to the content of Religion a simple, clear, and logical expression, but, on the other hand, it has preserved Christian doctrine from becoming a mere philosophy of Religion.*

Speaking exactly, we may say that Religion, when it has a sacred fundamental document, no longer requires Doctrine; for the content of the document is itself the Doctrine. But when the New Testament was created the Church already had a doctrine; indeed, as we have seen, this doctrine itself helped to create the New Testament. Doctrinal teaching could not be, nor ought it to have been, rendered superfluous and thrust aside by the new written work ; and it continued to be carried on in the Church. But all doctrine, however supernatural it may be in its foundations, depends for its exposition upon reason, and with the help of reason necessarily aims at simple and clear expression. As soon, however, as a sacred document comes into existence, doctrine begins to depend less and less on reason for its development ; for each rational element *can* now be replaced by an authoritative element. The consequence is that both rational and authoritative elements are intermingled in the development of doctrine, that everyone becomes accustomed to such intermingling, and that the sense and desire for clear and logical thinking gradually become dulled. All this is exemplified to full extent in the history of the development of Dogma in the Church. We may observe it already in Irenæus, in Tertullian with special clearness, and in Origen. They operate with *ratio* and with *autoritas*, *i.e.* with proofs from Scripture, and interchange the two elements at will. A text from the New Testament is for them as good a proof as a logical argument. The result for the dogmatist was a tremendous and increasing relief from logical responsibility, and a corresponding increase in the patchiness and incoherence of doctrine. If the dogmatist was at a loss for an argument, a passage of Scripture came to his help; if doubts arose in his mind, they were repressed by a word of Scripture; if a proof could not be found, it was supplied by a verse of Scripture; if discrepancies were met with, these need only be so in appearance, for Scripture contains discrepancies, and yet Scripture is absolutely consistent. This condition of things gradually affected Dogmatics, and with the narcotic of Scriptural authority paralysed the intellect in its restless search for truth. We can observe these evil effects in case of a great genius like Augustine; how much more quick and ready may lesser spirits have been to dispense with real consistency, perspicuity, and logical proof in their teaching of the Faith! In truth the Dogmatic of the Church is a creation that scorns logical stringency, and the dogmatist, if he only has given "the teaching of Scripture," can feel dispensed from what is his chief task.

But also from another side the New Testament paralysed the intellectual instinct to give to the content of religion simple and consistent expression. If *all* that stood in the New Testament must count as sacred and "written for our instruction," then indeed was it an absolutely hopeless undertaking to gather all this into a single system of doctrine. And if the whole varied content of the New Testament belonged to "Religion," then it was now an impossible task here to introduce arrangement and system. Thus the whole idea of Religion as an objective and subjective unity was obscured. Religion is everything that stands in the New Testament. How then can a sound doctrine of religion exist at all? However, fortunately, the intellect found a base of action in the Rule of Faith, and intellectual effort based upon the Rule of Faith proved stronger than the paralysing influence of the varied matter of the New Testament upon Dogmatics; and yet in hundreds of instances, and, indeed, from the beginning, the New Testament has exercised a disturbing, paralysing, and disintegrating influence upon Dogmatics.

And yet—here also there is another side to the account: *The New Testament has again and again brought Dogmatics back to history*, and has thereby preserved it from changing into mere Philosophy of Religion. We can observe the working of this influence from the first days, and even in the dogmatic developments of the nineteenth century it has continued to be fraught with blessing. What a different aspect the Dogmatic of Origen would have had—and indeed to its disadvantage—if he had not always kept himself in touch with the New Testament, if he had not felt obliged to speak in unison with that Book! If only separate works and not an already collected New Testament had been at his hand, his Dogmatic would have been much more neo-Platonic in its results than it already is. And what a debt Augustine, as a dogmatist, owes to the New Testament! Without the Gospels and the Pauline Epistles as *canonical authorities,* he would never have been delivered from the scepticism of the Academy nor would he have accomplished that deepening of the neo-Platonic philosophy by which he has transformed it in some of its speculations into pure religion. Thus though the Dogmatic of the Church be ever so patchy, incoherent, and self-discrepant in the form that it has taken, the fact that it has not completely lost contact with real life and history is due to the New Testament.

In the foregoing pages an attempt has been made to survey and set in order the most important consequences of the Creation of the New Testament. This task belongs to the historian of the Origin of the Sacred Collection—not only because practically all these consequences made their appearance with the Book itself, but also because from the consequences we can gain a clearer and more certain knowledge of the motives which produced the Book, and because in these consequences the real character of the Book first appears. It is true, as has been shown, that consequences do not always correspond to motives—a creation very speedily creates its own law and follows its own logic—but knowledge of the coming into being of the New Testament is imperfect so long as an account is not given of what really came into being in this case. Therefore it is much to be desired that, for the future, histories of the "Origin of the Canon of the New Testament" should not be written without a description of the innate functions and consequences of the factor introduced into the history of the Church by the appearance of the New Testament. The investigation of the history of the New Testament from Origen and still more from Athanasius downwards is, except in a few important points, only of interest to scholars; but to know what the New Testament meant to the Church as soon as it was created belongs to general theological culture.

APPENDICES

APPENDIX I (to § 2 of Part I, pp. 59 f.)

The Marcionite Prologues to the Pauline Epistles

(*The most ancient authority is Codex Fuldensis, but they also appear in at least thirteen other Codices*)

Gal.—Galatæ sunt Græci[!]. hi verbum veritatis primum ab apostolo acceperunt, sed post discessum eius temptati sunt a falsis apostolis, ut in legem et circumcisionem verterentur. hos apostolus revocat ad fidem veritatis scribens eis ab Epheso.

Cor.—Corinthi sunt Achaici. et hi similiter ab apostolo audierunt verbum veritatis et subversi multifarie a falsis apostolis, quidam a philosophiæ verbosa eloquentia [better: ad phil. verbosam eloquentiam], alii a secta [better: ad sectam] legis Judaicæ inducti sunt. hos revocat apostolus ad veram evangelicam sapientiam scribens eis ab Epheso per Timotheum.

Rom.—Romani sunt in partibus Italiæ. hi præventi sunt a falsis apostolis et sub nomine domini nostri Jesu Christi in legem et prophetas erant inducti. hos revocat apostolus ad veram evangelicam fidem scribens a Corintho.

Thess.—Thessalonicenses sunt Macedones. hi accepto verbo veritatis perstiterunt in fide etiam in persecutione civium suorum ; præterea nec receperunt ea quæ a falsis apostolis dicebantur. hos conlaudat apostolus scribens eis ab Athenis.

Laudic. (=Eph.).—[Laudiceni sunt Asiani. hi præventi erant a pseudo-apostolis . . . ad hos non accessit ipse apostolus . . . hos per epistulam recorrigit. . . .]

Col.—Colossenses et hi sicut Laudicenses sunt Asiani, et ipsi præventi erant a pseudo-apostolis, nec ad hos accessit ipse apostolus, sed et hos per epistulam recorrigit ; audierunt enim verbum ab Archippo qui et ministerium in eos accepit. ergo apostolus iam ligatus scribit eis ab Epheso.

Phil.—Philippenses sunt Macedones. hi accepto verbo veritatis perstiterunt in fide nec receperunt falsos apostolos. hos conlaudat scribens eis a Roma de carcere per Epaphroditum.

Philem.—Philemoni familiares litteras facit pro Onesimo servo eius ; scribit autem ei a Roma de carcere.

These Prologues were first recognised as really Marcionite by De Bruyne (*Rev. Bénéd.*, 1907, Jan., pp. 1–16), who thus made a particularly important contribution to our knowledge of the history of the New Testament. He has absolutely proved that these Prologues belong together (those to the Pastoral Epistles are of a different character); that they are to be ascribed to the Marcionites; and from them came into the Church.[1] The uniform character of the Prologues, taken in conjunction with the fact that "lex et circumcisio" (Gal.)="lex et prophetæ" (Rom.)="secta

[1] This view is accepted by Wordsworth-White (*Novum Testamentum Latine*, ii. 1, 1913, pp. 41 f.).—The order of the ten epistles was here originally, as the discoverer has acutely shown, that of the Marcionites.

legis Judaicæ," suffices to assure us on this point. The Prologues accordingly reject as false the Christianity that upholds the Old Testament, and call the great Church a Jewish sect. They evidently identify the original Apostles, or all missionaries of their party,[1] with the Jewish opponents of St Paul, and describe as false every mission before that of St Paul. Where such missions had taken place, Paul must "revocare" or "recorrigere" (Rom., Laod., Col.). Where missions had followed him, he must likewise "revocare" (Gal., Cor.). It is, however, especially characteristic that all the epistles (except the epistula familaris to Philemon) have been searched only for information as to the attitude of the respective Churches towards the "verbum veritatis" (Gal., Cor., Thess., Phil.) or to the "fides veritatis" (Gal.), the "vera evangelica sapientia" (Cor.), the "vera evangelica fides" (Rom.), and the "fides" (Thess., Phil.). Under these suitably varying expressions Pauline Christianity (assumed to be independent of the Old Testament) is always to be understood.[2] This point of view is simply imposed upon Thessalonians and Philippians. In the Prologue to Colossians "verbum" without the epithet "veritatis" probably means the false Gospel.

These Prologues show that the Marcionite "Apostolus" influenced the "Apostolus" of the Church, and one feels that this must have happened at a very early period. They have not yet been found in Greek

[1] The false apostles that, according to the prologue to Cor., "multifarie" led astray the Corinthians, are certainly in the first place Peter and Apollos.

[2] We note by the way that "veritas" ("verus") is a genuine Marcionite watchword, derived from the Epistle to the Galatians, the most important epistle for Marcion (Gal. ii. 5: ἡ ἀλήθεια τοῦ εὐαγγελίου).

form ; but something can be said in favour of a Greek original. The notices concerning the places where each letter was written deserve attention seeing that they are so ancient. Since Philippians and Philemon are described as having been written from Rome, it is allowable to question whether the words in the prologue to Colossians : " Apostolus ligatus (surely the Roman captivity is meant) scribit eis ab *Epheso* " are in order, although they do suit an hypothesis that has been revived only lately that Colossians was written in Ephesus. Perhaps we should read "a Roma per Epaphram " (confusion of " Epaphras " and " Ephesus "). These Prologues were not written for the educated, but for quite simple people ; the writer even thinks it necessary to write : " Romani sunt in partibus Italiæ." No Western could have done this. The geographical notices would suit the hypothesis that the Prologues were originally composed for Christians of Pontus.

APPENDIX II (to § 1–4 of Part I)

FORERUNNERS AND RIVALS OF THE NEW TESTAMENT

THOSE collections of authoritative Christian works that, according to early indications in the course of the development of the New Testament, might have come into existence but have not come down to us, call for thorough investigation; here let it suffice to give a list of them accompanied by some words of explanation. Something has already been said about them in the text of this book. I count *seven* of these embryonic collections :—

1. A collection of late Jewish and Christian prophetic-messianic or prophetic-hortatory books inserted in the Old Testament—thus an expanded and corrected Old Testament.

2. A collection of (late Jewish and) Christian prophetic books standing independently side by side with the Old Testament.

3. A simple collection of Sayings of the Lord, like the common source of St Matthew and St Luke (*Q*), standing side by side with the Old Testament.

4. A written Gospel, or a collection of several Gospels containing the history of the Crucified and Risen Lord, together with His teaching and commands, standing side by side with the Old Testament.

5. A Gospel (or several), with in addition a more or less comprehensive collection of inspired Christian works of the most different character and graded prestige, standing side by side with the Old Testament.

6. A systematised "Teaching of the Lord" administered by the "Twelve Apostles" of the character of the "Apostolic Canons, Constitutions, etc.," which also included "Injunctions of the Lord," side by side with the Old Testament and the Gospel.

7. A book of the synthesis or concordance of prophecy and fulfilment in reference to Jesus Christ, the Apostles, and the Church, standing side by side with the Old Testament.

It can still be shown that in the second century each of these "New Testaments," or additions to the Old Testament, not only were possible, but were already actually present in embryo; and further it can be shown why they did not come to full life, or perished.

1. Still, even at the end of the second century, Tertullian was of the opinion that the Book of Enoch must be included in the Old Testament; this book as well as the Apocalypse of Ezra, the Assumpsion of Moses and others were not only read by Jewish Christians, but had also penetrated to Gentile Christians, and were reverenced by them as books of revelation, as is proved by numerous quotations from these works (first and second centuries).[1] Christians took upon themselves to correct the Old Testament and even to interpolate whole verses (*vide* Justin, *Dial. c. Trypho*). Christian Apocalypses attained the highest prestige as soon as they were published. It was accordingly to be expected that, as the simplest way of developing the *litera scripta* given in the Old Testament, the ancient Canon would be enlarged by the addition of new works, and

[1] The Shepherd of Hermas quotes only *one* sacred work, the *Revelation of Eldad and Modad*, a work that is quite unknown to us.

that thus in the most obvious way the whole Canon might have been declared to be the property of Christians and not of Jews. This was, indeed, very nearly being done, and the inclusion of the Shepherd of Hermas in many (Western) exemplars of the Old Testament, *even in the Middle Ages*, may count as an important relic of this tendency. The possibility of giving the Shepherd a place in the Old Testament is considered even in the Muratorian Fragment, but is rejected *because the Old Testament is closed*. From the fact that this reason is stated so emphatically, we may probably conclude that it was not yet clear to everyone. The growing demand for books of the "New Covenant"—corresponding to the increasing perception in the Church of the limitations of the Old Covenant—and the new attitude that the Church was compelled to adopt towards prophecy since the middle of the second century, repressed the tendency that would have realised itself in No. 1.

2. It was also conceivable that the prophetic books to be added to the Old Testament should form a Canon *of their own*. The difference from No. 1 would not have been very great, yet it would have been considerable; for the idea of a second Canon would have been formed and realised—an idea that implied an enhanced Christian self-consciousness. The new Canon would have expressed the feeling that Christians found themselves living in a new epoch (*vide* Acts ii. 17 f.), wherein "the Spirit was poured upon all flesh, even upon the servants and handmaids." The Book of Revelation makes the strongest claim to be regarded as an authoritative prophecy and presupposes that it would be read by the Churches; but one cannot imagine that its author ever intended that his book

should be inserted in the Old Testament; he surely meant that it should stand side by side with that book.[1] Tertullian's attitude towards the Montanist collection of prophecies is very significant. The New Testament was already in existence for him, and yet he wishes the Montanist collection to be attached to the "Instrumentum" of the Church: the thought of a new prophetic Canon is to him not repellent, but simply natural. (More details will be given in Appendix III.) If he had not had to reckon with a New Testament already in existence, it follows that he would have wished the new prophetic collection to be added to the Old Testament as a second Canon. A foundation for this idea, therefore, must have existed from primitive times. The same considerations and influences that made No. 1 impossible have prevented us from receiving the new Canon in the form of No. 2: prophecy as such had fallen in value when compared with what was historic and apostolic.

3. Very soon—indeed during Apostolic times and in Palestine—the primitive formula of authority the "Scriptures and the Lord" was recast so that "the Lord" found expression in a loosely ordered collection of Injunctions and Sayings of the Lord (*Q*). For a time the Churches were satisfied with this. But though the simple conception of "The Scriptures and the Lord," as the final appeal, was very tenacious of life—it can be traced even into the fourth century as if no New Testament were in existence—yet it very soon became manifest that the expression of the term "the Lord"

[1] According to the Apocalypse, one is to hear "what the Spirit saith" (*i.e.* caused to be written). This is an entirely new form, which could very well give the fundamental principle of a new canon side by side with the Old Testament.

in the form of a single collection of Sayings was insufficient, and it was soon displaced by No. 4.[1]

4. "The Old Testament and the (written) Gospel," or "the Old Testament and the written (four) Gospels": for a time it seemed as if such an arrangement would have sufficed for all. Most probably all Churches passed through this stage, and, according to the "Didaskalia" preserved in Syriac, it lasted in certain Eastern Churches up to the middle of the third century. In the "Gospel" or the "Gospels" was included the story of the Crucified and Risen Lord together with His teaching and injunctions (in some also with a preliminary history). This arrangement of the *litera scripta* seemed to satisfy all needs, and from many points of view we can regret that the Churches did not abide by it. We have already shown (pp. 42 ff.) what were the requirements and considerations that urged the Churches to a further step.[2] From these we also learn that the advance was not by any means altogether detrimental.

5. The characteristic of this form is that although the idea of a collection of books of the "New Covenant" in addition to the Gospel (the Gospels) has at last been realised, yet no clearness prevails as to the principle according to which further authoritative books are to be added to the Gospels. *The second half of the collection is still quite formless and is therefore destitute of boundaries,*

[1] In an undercurrent in the Church—even into the Middle Ages—"the Lord" still continued to be essentially represented by His Sayings and Parables, and lived especially in the Sermon on the Mount and the "Evangelical Counsels."

[2] What was needed was the collective testimony of the Apostles as a defence against heresy. But a no less decisive consideration was the fact that the Pauline Epistles, because of their wide circulation and their own weight, had become indispensable.

nor is it closed against other works. So long, however, as it was formless it was in an insecure and dangerous position. The principle of the Apostolic is not yet accepted or is not yet applied strictly. This is the condition of things presupposed by Clement of Alexandria and also by the Catalogus Claramontanus [1]; like all amorphous things it could not last and was defenceless against all kinds of questionable additions,[2] and so the formless was gradually replaced everywhere by the *formed* New Testament.[3]

6. The idea that led to this form of an authoritative Christian *litera scripta* is the most daring, most independent, and most interesting of all. It continued to assert itself in the Church even after the creation of the New Testament, indeed it experienced a still further development, and up to the present day has not been disavowed in the Catholic Churches. Accordingly even to-day the New Testament has a rival at its side, a rival that now, indeed, (and for a long time

[1] The same condition is also presupposed by the formula used once by Tertullian in one of his earlier writings (*De Præsc.*, 40): "Instrumenta divinarum rerum *et sanctorum Christianorum.*" I conjecture that this formula was current in Carthage immediately before the time of Tertullian, and that he referred to it once only as it were by accident. Still more important in this connection is the testimony that the collection of Pauline Epistles stood as a completely separate entity beside the Holy Scriptures (*Mart. Scil.*, *cf.* also the *Fragments of Caius*).

[2] An example is afforded even by the Muratorian Fragment in the strange addition of the "Sapientia," and by the Catalogus Claramontanus in the addition of the Acta Pauli.

[3] In so far as in later times the decisions of the Great Councils were proclaimed to be canonical, and were attached to the New Testament, this may be interpreted as an instance of the persistence of the idea that is expressed in No. 5, namely that the second half of the new collection is not closed but is still capable of additions of sacred and authoritative character.

past) must be contented with a more modest *rôle*, yet a recognised rival. This rival is older than the New Testament, for already at the beginning of the second century or somewhat later it appeared on the stage in the "Didache," *i.e.* "The Teaching of the Lord by the Twelve Apostles" (which some say dates from the end of the first century). This Apostolic Teaching of the Lord professes to give the ethical commands of the Lord and His authoritative directions for the ordering of the life and worship of the Church. The author depends partly upon the Gospel, partly upon late Jewish forms of catechetical instruction interpreted in the sense of the Sermon on the Mount, and for the rest he ventures to trace back the ordinances, that had taken form in the Churches, to the Lord through the Apostles, because he is convinced of their authenticity. An undertaking, indeed, that was as practical as it was daring! But, unfortunately, further developments became infected by the spirit of deceit, indeed of falsehood. All these were codified by the Church in the firm conviction that her principles, all that she had, all that she required, had been granted and would be granted to her by the Lord through the Apostles. At that time and for centuries afterwards the Churches did what is now done only by the Pope! *This procedure*—it was in fact nothing else than the codification of Tradition—*if it had been everywhere accepted might have rendered the New Testament, or at least the "Apostolus," quite superfluous.* This literature did, indeed, gain increasing acceptance; but because it never could give the same impression of unassailable authenticity as did works Apostolic in form and title, and because it, for some unknown reason, never found its way into public lection, it could not hinder the development of the New

Testament or, rather, of the "Apostolus." And yet it kept a place side by side with the New Testament, and thus from the Didache, or rather from the idea that lay at the root of the Didache, arose that great body of pseudonomous Apostolic literature of Canons and Constitutions. In this literature—the history of which and of its varying prestige in the Church has not yet been sufficiently investigated—the Apostolic Canons then attained such a prominent position that they were recognised in due form as Apostolic by the Catholic Churches, and actually took their place beside the New Testament; while the ancient Didache, at first included in the formless second division of the Holy Scriptures in Egypt, was since the time of Origen and under his influence thrust ever nearer to the edge of the precipice. At last it was pushed over after it had for some time lasted as a textbook in the religious instruction of catechumens (according to the direction of Athanasius).[1]

7. There was also a possibility that the Church might have received a book of the synthesis or concordance of prophecy and fulfilment in place of the New Testament. First attempts towards such a work are plainly enough

[1] If the Didache, or the idea which led to it, had firmly established itself, it would have entirely prevented the formation of the Apostolus, *i.e.* of the second part of the New Testament. We should have then received a canonical *litera scripta* in three divisions: (1) The Old Testament; (2) The Gospel (or the Gospels); (3) The teaching of the Lord through the Apostles. This third division would not have remained stable (as is shown in the actual history of these writings), but would have been subject to continual alteration and transformation in accordance with the continuous development of the Church; *for in essence it is nothing else than codified Tradition.* In fact the Catholic Churches still possess this third division, yet for the greater part in fluid and uncodified form. In the watchword "Scripture (Old Testament and New Testament) *and Tradition*" it has still a life of fundamental importance in these Churches.

discernible. Consider only those parts of Barnabas, of the writings of Justin (also of the pseudo-Justinian work, *De Monarchia*), of Tertullian (*Adv. Jud.* and *Adv. Marc.*, ii., iii.) that deal with such concordance. Such a work could have satisfied, so it seems, all present requirements that were not satisfied by the Old Testament; for if all prophecies referring to Christ, His Apostles, and the Church with her institutions (Baptism, the Lord's Supper, etc.) had been collected from the Old Testament and set side by side with instances of their fulfilment, Christians would have had a book of catechetical instruction together with the necessary historical material. It is a remarkable fact that though such a work did not come into being because no one could put it into form (if a skilful author had appeared and had made such a collection, it would almost certainly have become canonical),[1]

[1] Some beginnings on the line of such a collection must have been made as is indicated by the works just mentioned which presuppose, it seems to me, the existence of collections of Messianic passages from the Old Testament. Already the speeches in the first part of the Acts give promise of the arrival of such a collection. Perhaps the Jews already possessed something of the kind. In the "Testimonies" of Cyprian, passages from the Old Testament and New Testament are collected together for every dogmatic "locus." As the Testimonies enjoyed for a time a semi-canonical prestige, it follows that the synthesis of passages was also regarded as semi-canonical. *Vide* on the whole question the comprehensive and trustworthy work of von Ungern-Sternberg: *Die Traditionelle Neutestamentlichen Schriftbeweis "De Christo" und "De Evangelio" in der alten Kirche bis zur Zeit Euseb. von Cäsarea* (1913), and my critique in the *Preuss. Jahrbuch*, 1913, July, S. 119 ff. *Cf.* also Weidel, "Studien über den Einfluss des Weissagungsbeweises auf die evang. Geschichte" (*Theol. Stud. u. Krit.*, 1910, S. 83 ff., 163 ff.). Ungern-Sternberg has proved that the material which was employed for Scripture proofs was handed down in a *definite* though elastic form and arrangement. On pages 258 ff. the aim,

nevertheless its opposite, the antitheses of Marcion, did actually come into being, and was accepted as canonical in an heretical Church. This work, which we may imagine to have been a large and comprehensive production, and which accompanied the New Testament of Marcion, aimed at proving the discordance of the Old Testament with Christianity at all points. The Marcionite Church, therefore, is itself a witness of the importance for the Church of proving the concordance, and that it was well within the limits of possibility that a work of this kind with *canonical* prestige should have been produced.

There were thus seven starting-points of development that could have led to collections of works competing with the growing New Testament, and in part these developments did not only start, but actually took definite form. It is in this connection alone that the full significance of the creation of the New Testament becomes clear. We see that it was not the only possible new Canon and that it developed as the consequence of difficulties, tendencies, and strivings of various kinds. It still remains to discuss briefly what it would have meant for the Church, and especially for the expression of "ius divinum" in the Church, if one of the other forms had established itself instead of the New Testament.

The New Testament, in the form which it attained, at once acquired a threefold significance for the Church. It is (1) the authentic, because Apostolic authority for the history of Salvation through Jesus Christ, and

significance, and use of this material are set forth in eighteen short paragraphs. Though this synthesis did not exist in fixed written form, it exercised an influence similar to that of a written work (S. 294 ff.).

as such, compels belief. (2) It fulfils what was foreshadowed in the Old Testament, and while recognising the Divine origin of that book yet assigns to it only a preparatory significance. It is (3) the "instrumentum divinum," *i.e.* the authentic codification of the Divine laws and ordinances to be observed by the Church and the individual Christian. From this point of view it gives equal weight to the word of Christ and to the word of the Apostles, but it also exercised a certain sifting criticism on the ordinances of the "instrumentum divinum" of the Old Testament.

Now if No. 1 had established itself there would have been only indirect documentary authority for the history of Salvation through Jesus Christ; here prophecy would have continued in the leading position, and only isolated notices and testimonies from the history of Christ, such as are found in early Christian prophetical works (*e.g.* the Revelation), would have found a place beside prophecy. Moreover, the distinction between the New and the Old Covenant would not have come to clear expression, rather most that is distinctive in the Old Testament would have been obliterated by means of allegorical interpretation. The same consideration would apply to the "ius divinum." The laws of the Old Testament and the new Christian laws, if such had, indeed, taken form within the enlarged Canon, would have become indiscriminately confused seeing that the former would have been spiritualised where necessary. *The New Testament, on the contrary, had the significance, which cannot be too highly valued, that it enabled the Church to set certain limits to the allegorical method of interpretation as applied to the Old Testament, and thus to give a fair opportunity for an historical understanding of the Old*

Testament.[1] If we had been left simply with an Old Testament enriched with Christian elements everything would have been overwhelmed by a mist of allegory and, besides, a harmful process of Judaising would probably have set in. Lastly, if prophecy had remained the sole form of expression of what was specifically Christian, religion would have inevitably degenerated into a wild and unwholesome emotionalism.

If No. 2 (a collection of Christian prophetical works side by side with the Old Testament) had established itself, the unfavourable consequences considered under No. 1 would, indeed, have been somewhat weakened—for the distinction between new and old would have been emphasised—but they would not have vanished. The *historical* element so essential to the new Faith would have remained here as weak as in No. 1, and, because all that is essentially Christian would have remained confined within the forms of prophecy, the danger of degeneration into emotionalism would have been still to be feared. It is nevertheless imaginable that the sharp distinction of the new Canon from the old might have produced a satisfactory recognition of the independent status of the new Religion.

If the development had come to a stop with No. 3 (the Old Testament and a collection of Sayings of the Lord like *Q*), the commands of Christ would have attained an extraordinary importance as "ius divinum." Standing alone and independently at the side of the Old Testament they would have acquired enormous force. But in that case the Universal Church could scarcely have come into existence, or at least would not

[1] The New Testament has preserved to a certain extent the letter of the Old Testament (in its historical significance), a service of no small value.

have continued to exist; rather a spirit of strict ascetic moralism would have acquired the upper hand, and Christendom would have probably become a great group of ascetic communities based upon the "ius divinum" given by Christ. Even if this consequence had not followed, it is to be feared that, with the solution of the problem given in No. 3, the Old Testament would have still held a position that would have placed Christianity in danger of Judaistic influence.

The latter danger would have been avoided if the development had advanced to the stage of No. 4 (the Old Testament and *one* Gospel or several) and had come to a stop there; for the authoritative history of the Lord wondrously born, crucified, and risen again [1] would have more than held its own against the Old Testament.[2] Neither would there have been any fear of an encroachment of Moralism in the form of the commands of Christ as "ius divinum"; for the Gospel of Salvation and of Faith would have repressed all tendency to mere moralism. And yet the appeal of the new order would still have been wanting in compelling force, because the idea of the New Covenant would not have been firmly seized. Moreover, if the new Canon had been confined to the Gospel (the Gospels), the Church in the course of her development in contact with the philosophic systems and religions of the Empire would have had no guidance as to her behaviour. This guidance was afforded by the "Apostolic" writings, above all by the Epistles of St Paul in spite of other difficulties that they presented. Without such guidance the Church most probably would have

[1] Tertullian calls this history "Originalia instrumenta Christi" (*De Carne*, 2).

[2] "Originale instrumentum Moysei" (Tert., *Adv. Hermog.*, 19).

fallen into perplexity that might even have overwhelmed her. She would also have been absolutely defenceless against all that falsely pretended to be "Apostolic tradition," and as such claimed obedience.

If the development had come to a stop with No. 5 (the Gospels and a varied collection of Christian writings, Apostolic and otherwise), we might imagine that already almost everything would have been attained that has been attained through the New Testament. But although in this case a large number of sacred books of authoritative and directive character stood side by side with the Gospel (Gospels), still they were not subjected to one uniform principle. It is true that the idea of the Apostolic played an important part in them, but this idea was not yet recognised as the sole guiding principle. Hence unsuitable and disturbing elements could establish themselves in the Canon, which was not yet closed even in idea, to say nothing of actual practice. If this condition had remained final, then not only would the Canon have been liable to continual additions of a questionable character, but there would have been continual uncertainty as to what was "ius divinum"; and the grand weapon against heresy would have lost its edge, for the idea of firm apostolic tradition in the form of *litera scripta* would have been wanting.

We have already discussed how things would have stood if No. 6 (Old Testament, Gospel, and "Teaching of the Lord through the Apostles," or "Apostolic Canons") had established itself. The situation, however, which has become actual in the Catholic Churches—namely, that the New Testament with its "Apostolus," together with "Apostolic Canons," count as sources of the "ius divinum"—is especially suitable for the purposes of these Churches, because these extra-Biblical Canons bridge the gulf between the Bible and unwritten tradition, affording the latter a kind of foothold; and at the same time they make it possible to introduce the same gradation of prestige into the conception of what is canonical in the sphere of the new Covenant, as had been already introduced in the relation of the New Testament to the Old Testament. The idea of degrees of prestige—an idea which, when applied to the "ius divinum," is still more paradoxical than when applied to the "ius humanum"—is quite indispensable to the Catholic Church for her kingdom in which worldly and spiritual elements are so closely intermingled. She needs the idea even for her dogmas, indeed, if she wishes to remain a Church of tradition and yet to dominate the present, if she would be uniform and at the same time give scope to individuality, she cannot manage without it.

In regard to No. 7 nothing definite can be said, because we cannot even imagine how things would have shaped themselves, if only a definitely fixed synthesis or concordance of Old Testament prophecy with the history of Christ, of the Apostles, and of the founding of the Church, had stood as the new Canon side by side with the Old Testament.

APPENDIX III

The Beginnings of the Conception of an Instrumentum Novissimum; the Hope for the Evangelium Aeternum; the Public Lection, and the quasi-Canonical Recognition, of the Stories of the Martyrs in the Church.

In the first section of his *Kanonsgeschichte* (Bd. i., S. 3–22) Zahn has tried to show that when Montanism arose in Phrygia the New Testament was already in existence; that the Montanists, however, added to it a third Canon in which a kind of Gospel (the Logia of the Paraclete), analogies to the Pauline Epistles, and an apocalypse were to be found. Zahn's thesis, in spite of all the learning that has been lavished upon it, is untenable in this form—especially in what concerns the contents of this "Scriptura novissima"—as I have shown in my work, "Das Neutestament um d. J. 200" (1889). It is, however, quite true that the Montanists very soon set up a collection of the Sayings of the Paraclete (spoken by Montanus, Maximilla, and Priscilla) and assigned to it a status of the highest honour corresponding to the final character of the mission of the Paraclete. Also the conception that the Paraclete stands to the revelation given in Christ and His Apostles as Moses stands to Abraham is earlier than Tertullian, and belongs to earlier Phrygian Montanism; in both cases Grace precedes and is followed after a certain period by the giving of a Law.

Seeing, however, that the Revelation in Christ and His Apostles was for the Church represented in a written work, was "Scripture," it became a problem for Montanist Catholics like Tertullian what status they were now to assign to the prophecy of the Paraclete. In his later treatises Tertullian, in controversy with heretics and psychics, is accustomed always first to argue from the Old Testament and New Testament as "Scripture," and then to appeal to an oracle of the Paraclete as an instance of the clearest and most conclusive character; *but he neither treats nor quotes the collection of oracles as "Scriptura."* He therefore—in spite of his reverence for the sayings of the Paraclete, and although they were embodied in a collection—felt himself compelled to refrain from formally adding them to the "Scriptura." It was not expedient to create a "third" Testament; for then the importance of the first coming of Christ would have been depreciated in a fashion that would have offended Tertullian's Christian conscience (the Paraclete *belongs* to Christ and is sent by Him). But even the *natural* solution, the adding of the new collection as a *second* part to the New Testament would have had its own great difficulties; seeing that the New Testament consisted already of two divisions, and that the collection of oracles could neither be included in the Apostolus nor could be treated as a third part of the New Testament (in the former case it would have lost something of its own peculiar significance, even in the latter case this would have been obscured). Accordingly Tertullian seems to have been satisfied with treating the oracles of the Paraclete, taken as separate sayings, as in a formless and indefinite way equal to or even superior to Holy Scripture.

And yet he was not quite satisfied. The collection of oracles could not be produced as "Testamentum"—for there were only two Covenants and two Testaments, the old and the new—yet the collection of oracles belongs to the "Instrumentum ecclesiæ." The Old Testament and the New Testament are the "instrumenta pristina" (*De Monog.*, 4; *De Resurr.*, 63),[1] but "noster auctor" (the Paraclete) has his "instrumenta" and the Church ought to acknowledge them. And these "instrumenta" include not only the oracles in which the Christian Law has now first come to clearer expression, but also the famous deeds of the faithful who have submitted to the direction of the Paraclete, the visions they have received, and the martyrdoms they have endured through His power. The commands of Christ and of the Apostles do not yet in every sense stand on the topmost heights—of this Tertullian had no doubt—because they are still affected by a certain spirit of accommodation, and therefore the deeds of Christians before the time of the Paraclete were as a rule infected by a certain imperfection; but now through the Paraclete the Church has arrived at the time of perfection. All that had made this time what it was, all that this time had brought

[1] In *De Monog.*, 4, the expression "evolvamus communia instrumenta scripturarum pristinarum" does not refer only to the Old Testament (the plural itself, and also what follows, render this improbable), but to both Testaments in distinction from the word of the Paraclete active in the present. The same is true of *De Resurr.*, 63: "Quia hæreses esse oportuerat, hac autem sine aliquibus occasionibus scripturarum audere non poterant, idcirco pristina instrumenta quasdam materias illis videntur subministrasse . . . sed . . . iam spiritus sanctus omnes retro ambiguitates et quas volunt parabolas aperta atque perspicua totius sacramenti prædicatione discussit per novam prophetiam de paracleto inundantem."

forth, must ever be shown forth to the Church in public lection and must be received into her "instrumentum."

This is the position that Tertullian takes up in the preface to the *Acta Perpet. et Felic.*, which has been already referred to (p. 28, note 2): "Si vetera fidei exempla in literis sunt digesta, ut *lectione* eorum et deus honoretur et homo confortetur—cur non et nova documenta æque utrique causæ convenientia et digerantur? . . . Viderint qui unam virtutem spiritus unius sancti pro ætatibus indicent temporum, *cum maiora reputanda sunt novitiora quæque ut novissimiora* secundum *exuperationem gratiæ in ultima sæculi spatia decretam* (here follows the passage from Joel). itaque et nos qui sicut *prophetias* ita et *visiones* novas pariter repromissas et agnoscimus et honoramus, *ceterasque virtutes spiritus sancti ad instrumentum ecclesiæ deputatas necessario* et digerimus et ad gloriam dei *lectione celebramus . . . et nos itaque quod audivimus et contractavimus, annuntiamus et vobis.*"

Just as, at the time when there was no New Testament in the strict sense of the word, the Pauline Epistles were added to the Holy Scriptures consisting of the Old Testament and the Gospels, and thus found their place in the "Instrumentum ecclesiæ," so now Tertullian would have the Church accept the oracles of the Paraclete and the records of the spiritual heroes of the new age into her Instrumentum—not as an addition to the New Testament, but as a fundamental authority standing side by side with it. The considerations which here influenced Tertullian were by no means wholly and specifically Montanist: I have indeed shown in my article, "Das ursprüngliche Motiv der Abfassung von Märtyrer- und Heilungsakten in der Kirche,"[1] how greatly the Church also was interested in the possession of documents testifying to the present influence of the Holy Spirit. In the Church this interest was satisfied by proving that the same spirit and the same power that once wrought in the Apostolic Age were still at work: nothing to the detriment of the prestige of the New Testament could ever arise from this. On the other hand, there is no doubt that Tertullian thought that the new elements which were to be added to the "Instrumentum ecclesiæ" (not to either of the Testaments) ought to have in a certain sense superior prestige—the oracles of the Paraclete, because they for the first time contained the Christian Law *sine ambiguitatibus* and absolutely apart from any tendency to accommodation; the Acts of the Martyrs, like that of Perpetua, because by this heroic story, that had not its peer up to that time in Africa, Tertullian is convinced that Christians of the present day, of the time of the Paraclete, if they followed Perpetua, *would transcend the Christians pristinorum temporum and would at last realise genuine Christianity.*[1]

[1] The importance of the Acta Perpetuæ—not only according to the view of Tertullian, but also for the African Church—can scarcely be exaggerated. The life of Cyprian was written by Pontius mainly to put Cyprian in the place of Perpetua (vide *Texte u. Unters.*, Bd. 39, 3), and Augustine finds it still necessary to write (*De Anima et eius orig.*, i. 12; iii. 12): "De fratre autem sanctæ Perpetuæ Dinocrite *nec scriptura ipsa canonica est* nec illa sic scripsit, vel quicumque illud scripsit, ut illum puerum sine baptismo diceret fuisse defunctum"; and: "Exempla quae te fallunt vel de latrone qui dominum est confessus in cruce vel de fratre sanctæ Perpetuæ Dinocrate, nihil tibi ad huius erroris sententiam suffragantur . . . ipsa lectio (*scil.*, Acta Perpet.) *non est in eo canone scripturarum, unde in huiusmodi quæstionibus testimonia proferenda sunt.*" Vincentius Victor, against whom Augustine is here writing, had thus appealed to the Acta Perpetuæ together with the Gospel of St Luke as authorities

Strange indeed! The New Testament was scarcely created, at all events was not yet completed, when the most eminent Christian of the West already perceived its defects! The Canon which was intended to show, and by its very existence to render tolerable the imperfection and the "shadow" of the Old Testament is itself also clouded with a "shadow" and is not yet perfection! And this because it contains ambiguities and is governed by a tendency to accommodation, but above all because it has not been able to show as its credentials that the people of God now stands under laws so unambiguous as to exclude all doubt and weakness. On the contrary it is evident that controversy upon controversy emerges in the Christian life, and that every weakness and laxity could cloak themselves with texts from the New Testament—often indeed with unreason, but often also unfortunately with good reason! And thus under the influence of the New Testament Christianity so far had arrived at only an imperfect development! Hence there was need of a new Scripture and this was actually in existence: it comprised on the one hand the directions of the Paraclete, and on the other hand documents like the Acts of Perpetua. The Paraclete had now led Christians "into all the Truth," and has told them "what they could not bear before"; and evident tokens are

for his doctrine. Augustine reminds him that the Acta Perpet. was not in the Canon, but in the second passage he expresses himself in such a way that we recognise that he counted these Acts to belong to the "Instrumentum ecclesiasticum" in the wider sense; for he testifies that a certain canonicity could not be denied to them. This is an answer to Ehrhard's objections (*Byzantin. Ztschr.*, Bd. 19, 3 [1910], S. 610 ff.) against my above-mentioned treatise concerning the Acts of the Martyrs. Ehrhard rejects the idea that these Acts form in a certain sense a supplement to the New Testament.

already present of the enthusiasm of the perfect life that He has now enkindled.

"Pristinæ scripturæ" (Old Testament and New Testament)—"prophetia nova cum documentis martyrum": this arrangement of authorities alone answered to what was now at work. A part of Christendom, including the greatest Western theologian, already saw a "Shadow" upon the new-born New Testament, and looked for an *Instrumentum Novissimum*—indeed fancied that they already possessed it! The fancy redounded to their honour; for it was the expression of their absolute moral earnestness and sincerity even in the face of the Scripture of the New Testament.

But still more strange! About the same time the most eminent theologian of the East, the obedient son of the Scriptures and their greatest champion and exponent, also notes a "shadow" on the New Testament. It is true that for him this work, which he regards as forming a literary unity with the Old Testament (*Πᾶσα ἡ θεόπνευστος γραφὴ ἓν βιβλίον ἐστίν*),[1] is exalted above all praise and is the deepest fount of the mysteries of God, yet he cannot but note that it is not in every sense final. In passages like 1 Cor. xiii. 9 f.; 2 Cor. xii. 4; St John xx. 25; Rev.

[1] (All inspired Scripture is one Book.) From the point of view of the history of the Canon there is scarcely any difference between Origen's and Tertullian's conception of the New Testament (apart from the extent of the Canon). Origen, like Tertullian, emphasises the Apostolic character of the New Testament (Prophets and Apostles=Old Testament and New Testament), subjects interpretation to the Apostolic Rule of Faith (*De Princip.* iv. 2. 2: *ὁ κανὼν τῆς Ἰησοῦ Χριστοῦ κατὰ διαδοχὴν τῶν ἀποστόλων οὐρανίου ἐκκλησίας*) and upholds a distinction in prestige between the Old Testament and the New Testament as well as the thesis that the Divine character of the Old Testament can only be proved by means of the New Testament.

x. 4, Scripture itself points beyond itself, thus there is still a promise of an "Everlasting Gospel" for the Spiritual Church. Origen, in his works, often deals with this "Everlasting Gospel" (Rev. xiv. 6), contrasted with which the Gospel that we possess belongs to the αἰσθητά and temporalia. In *De Princip.*, iv. 13 (25), he writes :

"Sicut in Deuteronomio evidentior et manifestior legisdatio declaratur quam in his, quæ primo scripta sunt, ita et ab eo adventu salvatoris quem in humilitate conplevit, cum formam servi suscepit, clarior ille et gloriosior secundus in gloria patris eius indicetur adventus, et in illo forma Deuteronomii conpleatur, cum in regno cælorum sancti omnes *æterni illius evangelii legibus* vivent, et sicut nunc adveniens legem replevit eam, quæ *umbram* habet futurorum bonorum, ita et per illum gloriosum adventum inplebitur et *ad perfectum perducetur huius adventus umbra.* ita enim dixit propheta de eo (Threni 4, 20) : 'Spiritus vultus nostri Christus dominus, cuius diximus quia *in umbra eius* vivemus in gentibus,' *cum scil. ab evangelio temporali dignius omnes sanctos ad æternum evangelium transferat,* secundum quod Joannes in Apocalypsi *de æterno evangelio* designavit." [1] The continuation is

[1] Hieron., *Ep. ad. Avit.* 12 : "(Origenes) dixit iuxta Joannis Apocalypsin 'Evangelium sempiternum,' *i.e.* futurum in cælis, tantum præcedere hoc nostrum evangelium quantum Christi prædicatio legis veteris sacramenta. . . ." Jerome's literal translation is as follows : "Sicut enim per umbram ('veritatem' can scarcely be right) evangelii umbram legis implevit, sic, quia omnis lex 'exemplum et umbra' est cerimoniarum cælestium, diligentius requirendum, utrum recte intellegamus legem quoque cælestem et cerimonias superni cultus plenitudinem non habere, sed indigere evangelii veritate, quod in Joannis Apocalypsi 'Evangelium' legimus 'Sempiternum,' ad comparationem videlicet *huius nostri Evangelii, quod temporale est et in transituro mundo ac sæculo prædicatum.*"

suppressed by Rufinus, but it is preserved by Jerome and Justinian.[1] *In Joh. I.* 7 (S. 12 Preuschen) we read: Τοῦτο εἰδέναι ἐχρῆν, ὅτι ὥσπερ ἔστι "νόμος σκιὰν" περιέχων "τῶν μελλόντων ἀγαθῶν" ὑπὸ τοῦ κατὰ ἀλήθειαν καταγγελλομένου νόμου δηλουμένων, οὕτω καὶ εὐαγγέλιον σκιὰν μυστηρίων Χριστοῦ διδάσκει τὸ νομιζόμενον ὑπὸ πάντων τῶν ἐντυγχανόντων νοεῖσθαι. ὃ δέ φησιν Ἰωάννης "εὐαγγέλιον αἰώνιον," οἰκείως ἂν λεχθησόμενον πνευματικόν, σαφῶς παρίστησι τοῖς νοοῦσιν "τὰ πάντα ἐνώπιον" περὶ αὐτοῦ τοῦ υἱοῦ τοῦ θεοῦ καὶ τὰ παριστάμενα μυστήρια ὑπὸ τῶν λόγων αὐτοῦ τά τε πράγματα, ὧν αἰνίγματα ἦσαν αἱ πράξεις αὐτοῦ[2] (*cf.* i. 14, p. 18).

In Rom. I. 4 (T. vi. p. 21 Lommatzsch) Origen's note on Rom. i. 2, 3, runs: "Utrum simpliciter accipi debeat evangelium per scripturas propheticas a deo repromissum, an ad distinctionem *alterius evangelii, quod æternum dicit Joannes in Apocalypsi,* quod tunc revelandum est, cum *umbra* transierit et veritas venerit et cum mors fuerit absorpta et æternitas restituta, considerato etiam tu qui legis! cui *æterno evangelio* convenire videbuntur etiam illi æterni anni, de quibus propheta dicit: 'Et annos æternos in mente habui,' eique adiungi potest et ille *liber vitæ* in quo sanctorum nomina scripta dicuntur, sed et illi *libri qui apud Danielem,* cum iudicium consedisset, aperti

[1] *Vide* Koetschaus' Edition, p. 344.

[2] (This we must know: That just as the Law contains a "shadow of the good things to come" that are made clear by the Law when it is preached according to truth, so also the Gospel—the ordinary gospel as it is understood by ordinary people—teaches a shadow of the mysteries of Christ. But what John calls the "Everlasting Gospel," which should properly be called the Spiritual Gospel, clearly delivers to those who have understanding "all things face to face" concerning the Son of God Himself, both the mysteries delivered by His words and the ineffable acts of which His actions were mystic symbols.)

sunt. . . . Si ergo cum apparuit nobis hominibus, non sine evangelio apparuit, consequentia videtur ostendere, quod etiam angelico ordini non sine evangelio apparuerit, illo fortassis, quod *æternum evangelium* a Joanne memoratum supra edocuimus."

The idea of a distinct "Everlasting Gospel" was indeed suggested to Origen by the passage in Revelation; but it is no mere devotion to the text of the Bible that is here at work in him. Rather he looks for an Everlasting Gospel (1) because it is absolutely clear to him that Christ must necessarily still have a great work to perform for the cosmic powers (the dæmons) and that this will stand in the "Everlasting Gospel";[1] (2) because the Gospel that we possess refers to this sphere of Time, wherein nothing quite perfect can come to expression and everything must be clouded by the shadow of the transitory,[2] hence we are to look for a final Gospel which will bear the same relation to the New Testament as this to the Old Testament; (3) because he, like Tertullian both in feeling and thought,[3] was forced to confess with sorrow that Christians did not yet live a truly moral life, and that it was not possible in this world so to live,[4] therefore a time must

[1] According to the testimony of Jerome and Justinian this argument appeared in the passage which Rufinus suppressed in his translation. *Vide* also the note just given on the passage from Romans.

[2] If Origen could have used modern terminology he would have been forced to say here and in connection with many other parts of his system: Even the New Testament is something that is *relative*. This truly great theologian needs only to be freed from the "scientific" presuppositions of his times, to which he was as a matter of course bound, to appear, both in his characteristic broadness of mind as well as in the many sidedness of his knowledge, a critical and constructive genius of the first rank.

[3] Very many passages in his homilies and commentaries prove this.

[4] The latter belief is foreign to Tertullian.

come "quo sancti omnes æterni illius evangelii legibus vivent." The laws of our Gospel are not yet quite perfect, and, therefore, the life of Christians is not yet quite perfect.

According to Tertullian the Montanist, there is an "Instrumentum Novissimum" transcending the New Testament and containing the final revelation for the Christian life (given by the Paraclete), and also containing records that testify to the actual existence of the perfect life (Acta Perpet.); in this "Instrumentum" the shadow which still lies on the New Testament has vanished away. According to Origen there is for Christians the expectation of the "Everlasting Gospel"—but only after their departure from this realm of Time—in which the shadow of the New Testament is removed, and through which the perfect life will first become possible. In this point the Church has not allowed either Tertullian or Origen to prevail; yet she, led by Tertullian's second impulse, but at the same time correcting it, at once began to collect histories of the martyrs and to read them in the public services side by side with Holy Scripture. Through this practice of public lection they acquired a quasi-canonical prestige. Any thought of endangering the authority of Holy Scripture was quite remote from this practice, yet it strengthened in the Church the consciousness that the same spirit that had created the two Testaments was still to-day working powerfully in the Church. "Stupebamus audientes tam recenti memoria et prope nostris temporibus *testatissima mirabilia tua* in fide recta et catholica ecclesia" (August., *Confess.*, viii. 6, 14, in reference to the Vita Antonii)—this was the feeling of Catholic Christians also in the third century when they read stories of the martyrs. These, too, were to serve as "Canon" for the practice of the Christian Life. "Instrumentum novissimum"—"Evangelium æternum"—"Historiæ Canonicæ Martyrum": more than a century must pass before the Christian came that wrote down the phrase so simple and yet so decisive for the deeper history of Christendom, wrote down, as if it were self-evident: "Homo fide, spe, et caritate subnixus eaque inconcusse retinens non indiget scripturis nisi ad alios instruendos" (August., *De Doctr. Christ.*, i. 39 [43]). This was in truth the message of the Paraclete, and the Everlasting Gospel!

APPENDIX IV

THE USE OF THE NEW TESTAMENT IN THE CARTHAGINIAN (AND ROMAN) CHURCH AT THE TIME OF TERTULLIAN

IN the works of Tertullian there lies a great body of material from which one may form a judgment as to the use and valuation of the New Testament in the Carthaginian Church. I do not mean the passages in which Tertullian himself makes use of the New Testament, but those passages in which he reports instances where passages from the New Testament were employed as proof-texts against himself by his adversaries the "Lax" or, in his later writings, the "Psychics." The "Lax" or the "Psychics," however, formed the majority of the Church, and had probably the body of clergy behind them, so that we thus actually learn the general attitude of the Church towards the New Testament.[1] The writings of Tertullian form our sole authority for such information concerning that special period, and herein, too, they have no small value for us. If we did not possess them it would have been at least doubtful whether the attitude of the theological writers towards the New Testament was not in advance of the rest of the Church, and that a quite different view prevailed in the communities.

[1] Tertullian is concerned with the Church in Carthage, but in his latest works also with the Church in Rome, which, led by her bishop, rejects Montanism, champions the practices of the "Lax," and uses her influence in Carthage.

That Tertullian really had the *majority* of the community against him is clearly shown by *De Virg. Vel.*, i., among other passages, where Tertullian confesses in the first sentence: "Proprium iam negotium passus meæ opinionis," *i.e.* I am again left in a minority and must go on fighting.

In collecting the following passages I have used all the works of Tertullian, so far as they contain appropriate material, with the exception of those written against heretics: hence *De Præsc.* and *Scorpiace* have been neglected. These works also contain, it is true, objections and deductions made by the community,[1] but they do not allow of being clearly distinguished from the objections and deductions made by heretics.

The first thing to be stated is that the community already treat the New Testament just in the same way as Tertullian himself, that is, they have the same ideas about the book and therefore apply the same method of interpretation to, and make the same demands upon the book as he. Thus they required that for each regulation in Christian Discipline a text of Scripture must be in existence[2]—this is, in truth,

[1] Tertullian expressly states (*De Præsc.*, 8) that not heretics alone but also "our people" appeal to St Matt. vii. 7 ("Seek and ye shall find") as a justification for following their impulse to pry into the mysteries of religion. Tertullian declares that the text only refers to the Jews, or, if it also refers to Gentiles (Gentile Christians), it has force only under distinct limitations.

[2] *De Spect.*, 3: "Quorundam fides aut simplicior aut scrupulosior ad hanc abdicationem spectaculorum de scripturis auctoritatem exposcit et se in incertum constituit, quod non significanter neque nominatim denuntietur servis dei abstinentia eiusmodi"; cf. *De Spect.*, 20: "Quam vana, immo desperata argumentatio eorum, qui, sine dubio tergiversatione amittendæ voluptatis, obtendunt nullam eius abstinentiæ mentionem *specialiter* vel *localiter* in scripturis

Tertullian's own opinion, but when he is in a difficulty he renounces it, and in his later works he falls back upon the Paraclete—thus the silence of Scripture upon any point is most significant, for instance: The Apostles cannot have been baptised,[1] because the Scripture says nothing about it; while Scripture condemns unchastity it does not deny the possibility of forgiveness, therefore we must accept the possibility,[2] etc. Again, they agree as to the right of unlimited combination of passages of Scripture: Because in Gal. i. 16, "Flesh and Blood" can be referred to Judaism, so also the "Flesh and Blood" of 1 Cor. xv. 50 can mean Judaism, and the latter passage is therefore to be interpreted: "Judaism cannot inherit the kingdom of God"![3] Further, it is allowable to take one's stand upon one single text and from this standpoint to regard all others as if they did not exist, or, in other words, to twist them into harmony. This practice drives Tertullian to desperation (*vide*, e.g., *De Pud.*, 16: "Sed est hoc solemne perversis et idiotis hæreticis, iam et psychicis universis, alicuius capituli ancipitis occasione adversus exercitum sententiarum instrumenti totius [of the whole Bible] armari"); but how often had he done the same thing!

The following passages of the New Testament are alleged by the community against Tertullian:

St Matt. ii. 1 ff. (*De Idol.*, 9).—Magi appear in the New Testament and are not blamed as such, hence Magic and Astrology are not forbidden to Christians.

determinari, qua directo prohibeant eiusmodi conventibus inseri servum dei." *De Cor.*, 2: "Si ideo dicetur coronari licere, quia non prohibeat scriptura."

[1] *De Bapt.*, 12. [2] *De Pud.*, 18. [3] *De Resurr.*, 50.

St Matt. v. 25 (*De Fuga*, 13).—From the words : ἴσθι εὐνοῶν τῷ ἀντιδίκῳ, it can be concluded that *in Persecution* one may, indeed is commanded to, come to terms with the adversary.

St Matt. v. 40 (*De Fuga*, 13).—From the words : "From him who takes thy coat keep not back thy cloak also," one may deduce that in times of Persecution one is allowed to mollify the oppressor by yielding to him.

St Matt. v. 42 (*De Fuga*, 13).—From the words : "Give to him that asketh thee," it can be concluded that one may save oneself from the persecutor by paying him what he asks.

St Matt. vi. 14 (*De Pud.*, 2).—The general direction, "Forgive," must be regarded as unlimited.

St Matt. vii. 1 (*De Pud.*, 2).—From the command, "Judge not," follows the duty of unlimited forgiveness.

St Matt. ix. 15 (*De Jeiun.*, 2).—It follows from this verse that one ought to fast only at the Passion season ("when the Bridegroom is taken away").

St Matt. x. 23 (*De Cor.*, 1 ; *De Fuga*, 1, 6, 9, etc.).—The Christian may, indeed ought to, flee at the time of Persecution ("Flee from one city to another").

St Matt. xi. 13 (*De Jeiun.*, 11).—The ordinances concerning fasting are abolished because the Law and the Prophets only lasted until John.

St Matt. xi. 19 (*De Jeiun.*, 15).—Seeing that Jesus is pictured as ἐσθίων καὶ πίνων, it is unworthy of a Christian to burden himself with food restrictions.

St Matt. xvi. 18 f. (*De Pud.*, 21).—The bishop of Rome has the right to regard the promise to St Peter as holding good for himself.

St Matt. xix. 14 (*De Bapt.*, 18).—Seeing that Jesus called the children to Himself, one may, indeed ought also to baptise them.

St Matt. xxii. 21 (*De Idol.*, 15; *De Fuga*, 12).—The text: "Render to Cæsar the things that are Cæsar's" may, and ought to determine the behaviour of the Christian in persecutions.

St Matt. xxvii. 19 (*De Cor.*, 9).—Since Jesus wore a crown of thorns, the wearing of garlands ought not to be forbidden to Christians.

St Luke i. 28 (*De Virg. Vel.*, 6).—Mary is here reckoned among women because she was *betrothed*, not simply as a female ("Blessed art thou among women").

St Luke iii. 14 (*De Idol.*, 19).—Seeing that John exhorts the soldiers, but does not denounce the soldier's profession, therefore the profession of a soldier is permissible to a Christian.

St Luke iv. 29 (*De Fuga*, 8).—From this and similar passages it is to be deduced that, as Jesus withdrew Himself from His persecutors, so also may Christians.

St Luke vi. 30 (*De Bapt.*, 18).—From the general instruction: "Give to everyone that asks thee," it follows that one must give Baptism to everyone that asks for it (thus Baptism ought not to be delayed).

St Luke vii. 36 ff. (*De Pud.*, 11).—From the story of the woman who was a sinner, it follows that forgiveness must be granted to the Christian even if he has committed deadly sin (sins against chastity).

St Luke xv. (*De Pud.*, 7, 8, 10).—By interpretation of the several traits in the three parables of the Lost Sheep, the Lost Piece of Money, and the Prodigal Son, it can be shown that these refer only to the

Christian that has sinned (and not to the heathen), and that therefore forgiveness must be imparted even to one who commits deadly sin.[1]

St Luke xvi. 9 (*De Fuga*, 13).—From the injunction to make to oneself friends by means of Mammon, it follows that one may use bribes at the time of persecution.

St John iv. 2 (*De Bapt.*, 11).—As Jesus did not Himself baptise, it follows that baptism is not absolutely necessary.

[1] One of these special traits is that the woman looks for the drachma in *her own* house. Tertullian himself had once laid stress upon this point (*De Præsc.*, 12). Elsewhere they bring forward the following points: In Scripture the sheep is everywhere the Christian, the flock is the people, and Christ is the Good Shepherd of His people; the sheep has thus been lost out of the fold; the light that the woman uses is the Word of God that shines in the house (the Church), also the *hundred* sheep, the *ten* drachmæ, the *broom*, all have their interpretation. The elder son is the Jew who grudges the Christian his reconciliation with God the Father. ("My opponents lay special stress upon this point.") The younger son cannot, however, be the heathen, he can only be the Christian, for "the injunction to repent does not apply to the heathen; for the sins of the heathen are not subject to repentance but are rather to be ascribed to ignorance, which is sinful in the sight of God only because of sin in nature; surely remedies are not used for those who are not in danger. Ground for repentance is only present where knowledge and will are implicated in the sin, where it is possible to speak of guilt and on the other hand of Grace; he alone can mourn, he only can be afflicted who knows what he has lost, and what he will obtain again if he offers his repentance to God, who naturally enjoins this more upon His children than upon strangers." Concerning these interpretations made by his opponents, Tertullian remarks (*De Pud.*, 8): "With very many interpreters of parables the case is much the same as with those who trim garments with purple. They think that they have brought the tones of their colours into true harmony and by their contrast to have produced a lovely effect, but when the body comes to be fitted with the garment and it is placed in the right light, then the discords clash and reveal the whole construction as a ghastly mistake."

St John iv. 5 ff. (*De Pud.*, 11).—The story of the Samaritan Woman proves that the Church ought to forgive even the grossest sins.

Acts iii. 1 (*De Jeiun.*, 2, 10).—Because Peter went up into the Temple to pray at the ninth hour, this practice should be copied by the Church.

Acts viii. 36 (*De Bapt.*, 18).—From the so speedy Baptism of the Eunuch, one must deduce that it is right and a duty not to delay Baptism.

Acts x. 1 f. (*De Idol.*, 19).—The centurion was converted, therefore the profession of soldier is permissible for Christians.

Acts xv. 19 (*De Jeiun.*, 2).—The Apostles at the Council did not wish to lay any heavy yoke upon Christians, therefore the ordinances of the Montanists concerning fasting are out of place.

Rom. ii. 24 (*De Idol.*, 14 ; *De Cultu*, ii. 11).—The name of God ought not to be blasphemed, therefore Christians, in order to give no offence to the heathen, should comply with the customs of heathen festivals and homes, or at least should not show open displeasure with what the heathen do.

Rom. xii. 15 (*De Idol.*, 13).—One must rejoice with those that rejoice, therefore the Christian may join in the public festivals.

Rom. xiii. 7 (*De Idol.*, 13).—As it says : ἀπόδοτε πᾶσιν τὰς ὀφειλάς, the Christian may, and ought to, pay the usual dues on the days appointed by public custom.

Rom. xiv. 4 (*De Pud.*, 2).—This verse stands in the following passage which Tertullian controverts : "God is good, indeed is the supremely good, pitiful, merciful, rich in mercy, which He prefers to all sacrifice ; He would rather the conversion than the death of the sinner; He offers salvation to all men, and especially to those that believe. Therefore, we the children of God must also be pitiful and placable, forgiving one another as Christ also has forgiven us, judging not that we be not judged. For to his own lord each stands and falls. Who art thou that thou judgest another man's servant? Forgive and thou shalt be forgiven."

Rom. xiv. 17 (*De Jeiun.*, 15).—The Kingdom of God is not eating and drinking, therefore the ascetic rules of the Montanists concerning food are in fault.

Rom. xv. 1 (*De Fuga*, 9).—From the injunction "to bear with the weak," it follows that one ought to be gentle with Christians who flee at time of persecution.

1 Cor. i. 17 (*De Bapt.*, 14).—Paul says that Christ had not sent him to baptise, therefore one can even omit Baptism.

1 Cor. v. 10 (*De Idol.*, 14, 24).—Paul does not desire that a man should go out of the world, and does not forbid intercourse with heathen, therefore a Christian may frequent heathen meetings, festivals, etc.

1 Cor. vi. 18 (*De Pud.*, 16).—Paul says that the fornicator sins εἰς τὸ ἴδιον σῶμα, therefore he does not sin εἰς τὸν θεόν.

1 Cor. vii. (*De Idol.*, 5; *Ad Uxor.*, i. 3; ii. 1 f.; *De Exhort.*, 3, 4; *De Pud.*, 1, 16; *De Monog.*, 3, 11).—This chapter is exploited to prove (1) the unrestricted right to marriage, (2) the right of second marriage, and (3) of marriage with heathen, etc.

1 Cor. vii. 20 (*De Idol.*, 5).—The injunction that each should abide in his κλῆσις justifies every Christian

in abiding in his trade, even if it brings him into touch with idolatrous worship.

1 Cor. viii. 8 (*De Jeiun.*, 15).—What Paul here says about food and eating puts Montanist asceticism in the wrong.

1 Cor. ix. 22 (*De Idol.*, 14).—" I am become all things to all men " can and ought to serve as a maxim of broadmindedness for the Christian in his converse with heathen.

1 Cor. ix. 24 (*De Spect.*, 18).—One may go to the games in the "Stadium," seeing that the "Stadium" is mentioned in the Bible.[1]

1 Cor. x. 25 (*De Jeiun.*, 15).—One may eat anything that is sold at the shambles ; one must deduce all the consequences of this permission, and these are straight against Montanist asceticism.

1 Cor. x. 33 (*De Idol.*, 14).—The Apostle's saying, πάντα πᾶσιν ἀρέσκω, ought to lead the Christian to the greatest accommodation in converse with heathen.

1 Cor. xi. 5 (*De Orat.*, 21 f. ; *De Virg. Vel.*, 4).—As in this passage women and not virgins are spoken of, there is no need for the latter to be veiled.

2 Cor. ii. 5–11 (*De Pud.*, 13–17).—Seeing that here forgiveness is granted to an incestuous man, the Church must treat fornicators and adulterers in the same way.

2 Cor. xii. 7 (*De Pud.*, 13).—The fact that the mes-

[1] This is a peculiarly characteristic piece of exegesis: "Quod si et stadium contendas in scripturis nominari, sane obtinebis." It depends upon the axiom, " We have no right to blame what is not blamed in Holy Scripture," an axiom which is already found in Irenæus, and is also employed by the "Lax" to defend magic and astrology (*vide supra* on St Matt. ii. 1 f.).

senger of Satan did not even spare Paul shows that deliverance into his power cannot mean eternal damnation.

Gal. iv. 10 (*De Jeiun.*, 14).—The Christian that observes special days as festivals, as do the Montanists, falls under the condemnation of the Apostle.

Ephes. iv. 27 (*De Fuga*, 9).—The warning: μὴ δίδοτε τόπον τῷ διαβόλῳ is neglected if one simply faces the devil when he is active in persecution; one must rather flee from him.

Ephes. v. 16 (*De Fuga*, 9).—The injunction: "Redeem the time because the days are evil," refers to right conduct in persecution, *i.e.* one must flee, one must bribe, etc.

1 Thess. iv. 11 (*De Idol.*, 5).—The command to work with one's hands justifies every Christian who remains in his trade, even if thereby he cannot avoid coming into touch with idolatrous worship.

1 Tim. i. 15 f. (*De Pud.*, 18).—The saying: "Christ is come to save sinners," obliges the Church to limitless forgiveness.

1 Tim. i. 20 (*De Pud.*, 13).—Hymenæus and Alexander are delivered to Satan ἵνα παιδευθῶσιν, thus deliverance to Satan does not always mean damnation.

1 Tim. iii. 2 (*De Monog.*, 12).—Monogamy is only demanded of a bishop, therefore other Christians can marry again.

1 Tim. iv. 3 (*De Jeiun.*, 15).—The description of heretics as those who "refrain from meats" applies to the Montanists.

1 Tim. v. 11–15 (*De Monog.*, 13).—The advice of the Apostle that the young widows should marry again hits the Montanists.

Tit. i. 15 (*De Cor.*, 10).—"To the pure all things are

pure "—thus one need not be over-anxious about avoiding what belongs to idols.

1 John i. 7–10 ; ii. 1 (*De Pud.*, 19).—From these passages it follows that even the Christian cannot avoid sin, and that the forgiveness of God through Christ is boundless (καθαρίζει ἡμᾶς ἀπὸ πάσης ἀδικίας). Christ is the advocate and mediator in regard to all sins.

Rev. ii. 20–22 (*De Pud.*, 19).—From what is said about Jezabel we may conclude that sins of whoredom admit the possibility of repentance and forgiveness.

Hermas Vis. v. (*De Orat.*, 16).—Hermas sat down after he had ended his prayer, hence Christians also should sit down after prayer.

Hermas Mand. iv. 3, 4 (*De Pud.*, 10).—These passages prove the possibility of a second repentance and the right to marry again.[1]

Acta Pauli (*De Bapt.*, 17).—The example of Thecla authorises women to administer Baptism.

These instances of interpretation on the part of the community have been collected from fourteen treatises, and though a few may have been invented by Tertullian, the great majority of them are "genuine." They prove :

1. That the New Testament, in same compass in which Tertullian knew and used it, lay before his opponents in the Church, *i.e.* the majority of its members ; [2]

[1] That the Shepherd of Hermas was used at the beginning of the instruction of catechumens is clear from *De Pud.*, 10.

[2] Notice especially the references to the Acts of the Apostles, 1 John, Revelation, and Hermas. It is significant that references to the Acts and Hermas are found already in the earliest works (*De Bapt.*, *De Orat.*, *De Idol.*). On the other hand it is not certain that the

2. That their valuation of the book, the principles of interpretation they employed, etc., were exactly the same as those of Tertullian,[1] however much they differed from him in the employment of those principles in particular cases. The New Testament stands for them as a Canon side by side with and of equal dignity with the Old Testament; it contains as a divine fountain of justice (" Instrumentum divinum ") laws of the Christian life that are absolutely valid, thus it contains the " ius divinum." At the same time his opponents, just like Tertullian himself, recognise a distinction in degree between the two Testaments to the advantage of the New (" The Law and the Prophets are until John "); and the grand conception " Evangelium expunctor totius retro vetustatis " (Tert., *De Orat.*, 1) is never disputed, rather it is confirmed by them;

3. That, though the general impression that we receive from these expositions is unfavourable, it is obvious, nevertheless, that Tertullian has only picked out those that were offensive to him, and that some of them are certainly to be preferred to interpretations which Tertullian himself gives. We also now understand why Tertullian clung to the sayings of the

community regarded the " Apostolus " as closed; indeed the reference to the *Acta Pauli* makes this supposition improbable for the earlier period.

[1] We must beware of defining Tertullian's attitude towards Holy Scripture simply in accordance with his controversial work *De Præsc.*; we must throughout also take his other treatises into consideration. According to *De Resurr.*, 3, in controversy with heretics about doctrine, one must take one's stand on " scripturis solis." The strongest expression that Tertullian ever used in reference to Scripture stands in *Adv. Hermog.*, 22: " Adoro scripturæ plenitudinem "; note, however, that he does not say: " Adoro scripturam."

Paraclete in order to get over the difficulty of the uncertainty and even " Laxity " of many commands in the New Testament.

We may then adopt as our conclusion : At least as early as the last decade of the second century there existed in the Church of Carthage (not only for Tertullian) a second Canon of Holy Scripture comprising two divisions treated as equal in dignity—Gospels and " Apostolus "—in compass essentially the same as that of the Muratorian Fragment, and in all probability with the " Apostolus " still open—open, that is, for genuine Apostolic works that might yet appear.

APPENDIX V

"Instrumentum" ("Instrumenta") as a Name for the Bible

Zahn (*Gesch. des Neutestamentlichen Kanons*, i. 106–111) has published a thorough investigation of the term "Instrumentum" as a title of the Bible; but in my opinion he starts from an incorrect premise, and gives to "Instrumentum," in connection with the Bible, a significance that is more general than is admissible.

On pages 105 ff., Zahn writes: "Tertullian preferred to render Covenant by 'Instrumentum.' (In our investigation) we must start from this fact, incidentally revealed by Tertullian, that it was the prevailing custom among his contemporaries to express by 'Testamentum' what he preferred to call 'Instrumentum.' There is, accordingly, no doubt that in this as in similar cases Διαθήκη lies behind both terms." He then discusses "Instrumentum" in ordinary use and its relationship with "Documentum"; he asserts that the term not seldom occurs in Tertullian in its original wider connotation, and in conclusion remarks: "We should do injustice to Tertullian if we suspected that the term 'Instrumentum' covers a conception of the significance of the Holy Scripture for the Church that is merely legal. The Holy Scriptures were for him by no means mainly documents that could be produced by the Church in her case against heretics (Zahn refers to *De Præsc.*); though, as a matter of course, they were authorities of the highest value for the Church." On page 109 Zahn speaks of the elasticity of the concept "Instrumentum" as applied to Holy Scripture.

Three theses are here brought forward: (1) that "Instrumentum" in Tertullian (and when used elsewhere in the Church) is equivalent to "Testamentum"; (2) that "Instrumentum," like "Testamentum," is a translation of Διαθήκη; (3) that in Tertullian it has not only the special significance, "a fundamental document to prove doctrine," but also a more general significance. All these three theses are in my opinion incorrect, as I shall now proceed to prove.

As for the first thesis, it is true that Tertullian writes (*Adv. Marc.*, iv. 1): "Duos deos dividit, proinde diversos, alterum alterius *instrumenti*, vel, quod magis usui est dicere, *Testamenti*." Here it is of course clear that Tertullian (and others here and there) spoke of "Instrumenta" while the usual term was "Testamenta." And yet it would be a mistake to assert that "Instrumentum" is an equivalent for "Testamentum." In cursory speech it *can* serve as such, but in itself it is not. This is most strikingly clear from the three following passages: in *Adv. Prax.*, 20, Tertullian writes: "Totum *instrumentum* utriusque *testamenti*"; in *De Monog.*, 4: "Secedat nunc mentio parracleti ut nostri (the Montanists) alicuius auctoris; evolvamus communia (to us and the 'Psychics') *instrumenta scripturarum* pristinarum (*i.e.* the Old Testament and New Testament)"; and in *De Monog.*, 7: "Vetera *instrumenta* legalium *scripturarum*." Tertullian thus speaks of the "Instrument of the two Testaments," and of the "Instrument of the Holy Scriptures."

"Instrumentum" cannot, therefore, be an equivalent for "Testamentum." This also means that we have already disposed of the second thesis which is in itself highly improbable, for how could anyone have arrived at "Instrumentum" as a translation of Διαθήκη? It is true that very remarkable translations are found in the Old Latin of the Church. Why was not "Fœdus" rather than "Testamentum" used for Διαθήκη? Why was Μυστήριον translated by "Sacramentum," etc.?—but "Instrumentum" has no connection, or only the slightest, with Διαθήκη. Further, Zahn himself is compelled to confess that in quotations from the Bible Tertullian never translates Διαθήκη by "Instrumentum." Hence the term "Instrumenta" in reference to the Bible is just as independent of Διαθήκη as are the terms "the Holy Scriptures" or "the Books." The term, therefore, must have its origin in considerations that have absolutely nothing to do with traditional *names* for the Bible, but are concerned only with its *significance*—and, indeed, in considerations that are confined to the Western Church; for, so far as I know, throughout the whole range of the Greek Churches no equivalent for "Instrumentum" existed either in the second century or later.

We now come to Zahn's third thesis that the name "Instrumenta" for the Holy Scriptures is elastic, even if it approaches "Documenta" in meaning, and is not to be understood merely in a limited legal sense (documents to be produced by the Church against heretics). Here Zahn seems to be justified by the whole work, *De Præsc. Hær.*, in which Catholics are earnestly warned not to appeal to the Holy Scriptures when they dispute with heretics; therefore Tertullian cannot have regarded Holy Scripture as the fundamental document for doctrine. But it has long been recognised that Tertullian has been the very last man to heed his own warning, and that this whole work is a masterpiece of advocacy, a piece of special pleading, where the real heart of the author appears in his exposition of the Church's Rule of Faith. Now chance has so willed that the *only* passage in the works of Tertullian, in which "Instrumenta," as applied to the Bible, is simply and plainly defined as "instrumenta doctrinæ," should be found in this very treatise, *De Præsc.* Here we read in chapter 28: "Illic et scripturarum et expositionum adulteratio deputanda est, ubi *doctrinæ* diversitas invenitur. quibus fuit propositum aliter *docendi*, eos necessitas coëgit aliter disponendi *instrumenta doctrinæ*. alias enim non potuissent aliter *docere*, nisi aliter haberent *per quæ docerent*. sicut illis non potuisset succedere correptula *doctrinæ* sine corruptula *instrumentorum eius*, ita et nobis integritas *doctrinæ* non competisset sine integritate *eorum* per quæ *doctrina* tractatur." There can be no doubt here: The Holy Scriptures are here called "instrumenta," because they are fundamental documents, with whose help alone doctrine can be expounded and by which it is proved; "instrumenta" and "per quæ doctrina tractatur" are for Tertullian identical conceptions. Naturally the exposition need not always have a polemical character; rather it is true also for the Church that she must in behalf of her own knowledge prove her doctrine "per instrumenta Scripturarum"; so that the idea of a document is always implied in such proof. The Holy Scriptures are called "Instrumenta," because they are for the Church the decisive documents for the exposition and the proof of her doctrine.

A survey of the passages in which Tertullian uses

" instrumentum " will establish my position more clearly.

Naturally not a few cases also occur in Tertullian of the use of the word in a quite general sense. For instance he writes :

De Resurr., 63.—" Anima habet *instrumentum*, habet cultum, habet mancipium suum carnem."

Apol., 17.—" Tota moles ista (the world) cum omni *instrumento elementorum.*"

Ad Uxor., 1.—" Continentia ad *instrumentum æternitatis* (pertinet)."

De Cor., 8.—" Communia *instrumenta exhibitionis* (vitæ) *humanæ.*"

Again it is found in connection with the Conception " Literature " in general, and here it acquires the idea of a declarative and authoritative document :

De Idol., 10.—" Litteratura *instrumentum* est *ad omnem vitam.*"

Apol., 19.—" Multis *instrumentis* adsidendum est, reserenda antiquissimarum etiam gentium *archiva* " —here the close relationship of " instrumenta " and " archiva " is noteworthy.

Apol., 10.—" Si conscientia inficias ieret, de suis *antiquitatum instrumentis* revincetur."

De Cor., 7 (The question is concerning the origin of garlands).—" Litteræ ad hoc sæculares necessariæ ; de suis enim *instrumentis* sæcularia *probari* necesse est."

De Spect., 5 (The question is concerning the origin of the games, this must be investigated)—" de *instrumentis ethnicalium litterarum.*"

De Testim., 1.—The works of philosophers and poets are the " *proprium instrumentum* " of the heathen from which their teachings are known.

Scorp., 15.—"Si fidem commentarii voluerit hæreticus, *instrumenta* imperii loquentur ut lapides Hierusalem. 'Vitas Cæsarum' legimus." This use coincides with the common use of the period, especially with the use of the word in the sphere of civil and criminal law. Here it was quite usual to speak of "instrumenta publica, imperii, litis" (*vide* the Digests, Quintilian, Suetonius; Dirksen, *Manuale Lat. Font. Jur. Civ. Rom.*, p. 484, etc.), indeed it may be said that here also "Instrumenta," applied to written records, always includes the idea of declarative and authoritative document, of archives as a source of right; at all events the burden of proof lies with him who denies this. I know only one passage in Tertullian where the addition of "doctrina" does not seem to be permissible; *De Pud.*, 1, speaks of "instrumentum prædicationis"; but on closer view one finds here also that it is a question of "prædicatio doctrinæ."

In the passages now to be mentioned the concept "doctrinæ" either must be supplied to "instrumenta" or is at least not excluded.[1] We incidentally remark that the expression "Instrumentum" was so useful because it could be applied to the whole Bible, to each of the two parts, to groups of books, to separate books, and even to separate sections of the books.[2]

[1] Even when "instrumentum" is coupled with a genitive like "litteraturæ" or "ecclesiæ," the genitive "doctrinæ" can still always be supplied in thought.

[2] Just for this very reason the attempts that have been made by Roensch and others to divide the New Testament into separate parts in accordance with the use of "instrumentum" by Tertullian are altogether mistaken, for Tertullian's usage here is quite arbitrary, and in different places he groups the books differently. "Testamenta" can only be applied to the two divisions of the Bible, and is, therefore, to a certain extent handicapped by "Instrumenta."

It refers to the whole Bible in *De Præsc.*, 38; *Adv. Marc.*, iv. 1; *Adv. Prax.*, 20; *De Monog.*, 4 (passages that have been already quoted); also in—

De Pud., 16.—" Exercitus sententiarum *instrumenti totius.*"

De Resurr., 21.—" Tot ac talia *instrumenta divina.*"

De Pud., 10.—" *Divinum Instrumentum.*"

Adv. Marc., v. 1.—" *Omnia* apostolatus Pauli *instrumenta* " (all the sacred writings with the exception of the Pauline Epistles, which could not be used in this argument).

Acta Perpet., 1.—" *Instrumentum ecclesiæ.*"

It refers to the New Testament in :

De Præsc., 38.—" *Integrum instrumentum.*"

It very frequently refers to the Old Testament, because the Old Testament played the chief part as a proof-document. Instances are :

Apol., 18.—" *Instrumentum litteraturæ* " (of the Old Testament as a proof-document).

De Cultu, i. 3.—" Omne *instrumentum Judaicæ litteraturæ.*"

Apol., 21.—" *Antiquissima Judæorum instrumenta.*"

Apol., 47.—" *Vetus Instrumentum.*"

Ad Hermog., 20.—" Evangelium supplementum *instrumenti veteris.*"

Apol., 19.—" *Instrumentis* istis *auctoritatem* suam *antiquitas* vindicat."

De Pud., 7.—" Lex et prophetæ=*instrumenta.*"

De Monog., 7.—" *Vetera instrumenta legalium scripturarum.*"

Adv. Marc., v. 1.—" *Instrumentum creatoris* " (the Old Testament).

" Instrumentum " is applied to separate books and groups of books in the following passages :

Adv. Hermog., 19.—" *Instrumentum* originale *Moysei* " (cf. *Adv. Marc.*, i. 10).

De Resurr., 33.—" *Propheticum instrumentum.*"

Adv. Marc., iv. 10.—" *Instrumentum Danielis.*"

Adv. Marc., iv. 2.—" *Evangelicum instrumentum.*"

De Resurr., 39, 40; *De Pud.*, 12.—" *Apostolicum instrumentum,*" " *Apostolica instrumenta.*"

Adv. Marc., iv. 3.—" *Instrumentum apostolorum.*"

De Resurr., 38.—" *Instrumentum Joannis.*"

Adv. Marc., iv. 2; v. 6.—" *Instrumentum Lucæ.*"

Adv. Marc., v. 2.—" *Instrumentum Actorum.*"

Adv. Prax., 28 (*De Resurr.*, 39, 40).—" *Tota instrumenta Pauli.*"

Adv. Marc., v. 13.—" Instrumentum " in connection with the Epistle to the Romans; but it may also refer to the whole New Testament.

Lastly, " Tot originalia instrumenta Christi " in *De Carne*, 2, means the separate passages of the story of the Birth.

The name " Instrumentum " (" Instrumenta "), when applied to the Bible, *in idea* places this book above doctrine—for the Bible is thus made the source of, and documentary authority for, doctrine—but *actually* it does the reverse. It is a term borrowed by Theology from Law—and therefore so welcome to Tertullian—that ignores the chief significances of the Bible as a book of religious edification. We never find expressions like " Instrumentum lectionis " or " Instrumentum ædificandæ ecclesiæ," nor could such expressions well be used. It would have been most unfortunate if the name " Instrumentum "—" divinum " would probably have been added—had established itself; but there was no danger that this would happen for it never became a rival of the name " Testamentum."

The word is a creation of the ecclesiastical spirit of the West; as we have already remarked, nothing like it was known in the East.[1]

It is very remarkable that Cyprian always avoids the word as a title for the Bible, likewise Lactantius, and, unless I mistake, Novatian also. Cyprian was simply not a professed theologian and dogmatic controversialist. The Bible with him ministered to "instructio vitæ," while its significance as "instrumentum doctrinæ" fell quite into the background. Cyprian, the typical catechist, derives from the Bible "divina testimonia," which he also calls "magisteria divina" (*Testim.*, i., Præf.; iii., Præf.).

Still the name "Instrumentum" for the Bible occurs not seldom in Jerome, Rufinus, and Augustine. Optatus too speaks of "instrumenta divina legis" (i. 13; vi. 5).[2] Thus the juristic spirit of Tertullian and of the West still lived on; nevertheless, at last the title "instrumenta" fell into utter oblivion.

[1] Allied to "instrumentum" is the name "paratura" for the Bible, which Tertullian endeavoured to introduce without success; this term too belongs to the vocabulary of demonstration and controversy; vide *Apol.*, 47: "Nostra haec novitiola paratura"; *De Cor.*, 1: "Calceatus de evangelii paratura"; *Adv. Marc.*, iv. 3: "Paratura authentica"; *De Monog.*, 7: "Omnis nostra paratura"; *Adv. Marc.*, iv. 1 (*cf.* ii. 1): "Paratura Marcionis" (the Bible of Marcion).

[2] i. 37 (p. 30, 1): "Strumenta," not "instrumenta," is to be read.

APPENDIX VI

A Short Statement and Criticism of the Results of Zahn's Investigations into the Origin of the New Testament.

Following upon his great work, *Geschichte des Neutestamentlichen Kanons*, of more than 2000 pages, Zahn has published in his *Grundriss der Geschichte des Neutestamentlichen Kanons,* a short summary of the results of his investigations. On page 13 we find the sentence: "Unless there had been occasions for uncertainty as to the limits of the Bible (the New Testament) there would have been no history of the Canon." After this bold statement it must appear that, according to Zahn, the New Testament—like dogma for the Catholic Church—came into existence from the moment at which its latest book was published, and that there is such a thing as the "history" of the New Testament only, "because the Christian works that were used for public lection were not from the first absolutely the same *in all orthodox communities,*" "because, even in one and the same community, variations in this practice lasted for quite a long time," and lastly, "because *the conception of what should be regularly read at public worship had not been clearly defined,*" in so far as all kinds of works were read publicly that did not belong to the Canon. Finally, "Even among works inherited from the Apostolic age, differences, in respect of the frequency and regularity of their use in public worship, must have existed according as they were more or less suitable for religious instruction."

There is still need of a short discussion of the results of Zahn's criticism, because these results are often developed in a way against which the author himself must feel inclined to enter an energetic protest. We hear everywhere that Zahn, the most learned of the critics, has proved that the New Testament came into existence so early as the end of the Apostolic age, about the year A.D. 100; and that so-called critics of far inferior learning place the origin of the New Testament about a century later. Against such a position we would establish the following points:

1. The first part of Zahn's larger work, as well as his *Grundriss*, ought not to bear the title *History of the Canon of the New Testament*, but *History of the public and private use of works that were afterwards united in the New Testament*; in the second part also the question of public lection is very much to the front. *The right to be read publicly and the right to be included in the Canon are jumbled together by Zahn as if they were identical*, though he himself admits (*vide supra*) that the conception of what should be regularly read at public worship "had not been clearly defined." It is, indeed, quite true, that every work that was "Canonical" (in the sense of the Old Testament) was also read publicly, but the converse statement is simply inadmissible. Public lection was certainly a most important preliminary condition for the canonising of a book (in many cases, however, it was a consequence), but it was by no means the sole condition. I mean that because a book was read at public worship it is far from following that it had, therefore, the same dignity

as the Old Testament. But this is the very point! In so far, therefore, as Zahn, dealing with the earliest history of the "Canon of the New Testament," confines himself, and must confine himself, exclusively to proving the existence of certain smaller collections of books now in the New Testament and the fact that they were read publicly, his work is simply not a history of the Canon of the New Testament, but—even if all his investigations are correct and to the point—a history of the earliest public and private use of certain books. Moreover, it hangs together with this unjustifiable identification of public lection and Canon that Zahn, in his larger work, thinks that he may neglect all other aspects of the history of the origin of the New Testament. The most learned authority on the second century in his discussion of this question makes really no use of his knowledge of the opinions and controversies, of the problems great and small, that agitated the Christendom of those days. Hundreds of details in the history of that period are brought forward and investigated thoroughly and comprehensively, but the growing New Testament is never brought into connection with the living history of the Church—not at all because the author was unable to do this, but because he believes that it is not necessary—public lection alone is sufficient and decisive.

2. In the *Grundriss*, Zahn has divided the early history of "the Canon of the New Testament" into three sections: "The New Testament about A.D. 170-220"; "The New Testament about A.D. 140–170"; "Earliest Traces of, and the Origin of, Collections of Apostolic works."

The third section (*i.e.* the one dealing with the earliest period) ends (p. 40) with the following statement: "Many questions referring to the origin of the New Testament will always remain without a certain answer. Yet it may be regarded as certain that about the years A.D. 80–110, both the 'fourfold' Gospel and the corpus of thirteen Pauline Epistles were in existence, and had been introduced into public worship along the whole line from Antioch to Rome, and that these two collections which form the most important part of the New Testament were from the first surrounded in public worship and in the estimation of the communities by a larger or smaller circle of Christian works that, like the two collections, seemed suitable for reading at public worship with a view to the religious instruction of the communities." Here, indeed, much more is asserted than can be proved and than Zahn himself has proved; for I cannot see—even on the basis of Zahn's own investigations—what justification there is for going back to a date so early as A.D. 80, nor can I discover the evidence for "the whole line from Antioch to Rome," nor the authorities upon which Zahn rests his statement that the public reading of the Gospels and of the Pauline Epistles at that period is alike certain; indeed, I believe that Zahn himself, on closer reflection, would substitute the years A.D. 110–130 for A.D. 80–110 as more appropriate for what he asserts. However, supposing that he is justified in what he claims, what, after all, is proved thereby? Surely no more than this, that in some, perhaps in several, communities, public lections from the four Gospels and the Pauline Epistles were the custom. It is well that Zahn himself has refrained in this connection from letting his pen write the word New Testament, and it is also good that he has guarded himself from *naming* the Christian works, apart from the Gospels and the Pauline Epistles, that were publicly read at that time. He only asserts that at that time already other works were so honoured, and to this assertion no objection can be raised. Seeing now that he preserves absolute silence concerning the years A.D. 110–140, we must assume that during that period absolutely no change took place in the conditions that are supposed to have already existed between A.D. 80 and 110—this means that, *according to Zahn, we cannot prove that a New Testament, set on the same level as the Old Testament, existed during the period before* A.D. 140. The four Gospels were read publicly, the Pauline Epistles were read publicly, some other works were read publicly—that is all.

But Zahn does assert the existence of the New Testament, at all events, for the period A.D. 140–170. This section of his work bears the title : "The New Testament about A.D. 140–170," and he probably thinks also of certain deductions that can be made, not without justification, for the former period, though he does not enter into them. The evidence, however, that the New Testament was in existence in the Church during that generation is exclusively based upon the Bible of Marcion, the Bible of the Valentinians, and the writings of the Apostles in Justin. Here we would make the following observations : (1) in reference to Marcion it is, of course, as good as certain that he dealt as a critic with the four Gospels of the Church ; but all other questions—whether he knew of the Pastoral Epistles, whether he criticised the Acts of the Apostles or the Apocalypse, etc.—must unfortunately remain unanswered. As for the main question, however, whether he knew of, or assumes the existence of, a written New Testament of the Church in any sense whatever, in this case an affirmatory answer is most improbable, because if this were so he would have been compelled to make a direct attack upon the New Testament of the Church, and if such an attack had been made we should have heard of it from Tertullian. Marcion, on the contrary, treats the Catholic Church as one that "follows the Testament of the Creator-God," and directs the full force of his attack against this Testament and against the falsification of the *Gospel* and of the Pauline Epistles by the original Apostles and the writers of the Gospels. He would necessarily have dealt with the *two* Testaments of the Catholic Church if the Church had already possessed a New Testament. His polemic would necessarily have been much less simple if he had been opposed to a Church which, by possessing a New Testament side by side with the Old Testament, had *ipso facto* placed the latter under the shelter of the former. In fact Marcion's position towards the Catholic Church is intelligible, in the full force of its simplicity, only under the supposition that the Church had not yet in her hand any "litera scripta *Novi Testamenti.*" (2) In reference to the Valentinian school Zahn asserts that: "The New Testament, which from the productions of the most important Gnostic School of about A.D. 140 in all its ramifications, we learn to have been the common possession of the Church, was identical with the New Testament of about A.D. 200;" but in order to arrive at such a result the truth of many incorrect equations must be assumed. It is not necessary here to discuss all these; we would, however, just make only the following remarks: In the first place we must neglect all the information derived from the Fathers of about A.D. 200 who assert or assume the identity of the New Testament of the Valentinians with that of the Church, for it is a well-known fact that the Valentinians both kept in touch with the Church and also conformed outwardly to the progressive development of the times in things ecclesiastical ("communem fidem adfirmant"). Next we must give special prominence to Ptolemy's words (*Ep. ad Floram.*, 1, 9): "We shall prove our statement (concerning the Godhead, the Old Testament, etc.) from the Words of our Saviour; for with their help it is alone possible to arrive without stumbling at the understanding of reality."[1] Thus, according to Ptolemy, who like all Valentinians adopted a critical attitude towards the Old Testament, the Word of the Lord is the sole court of final appeal. His practice is actually in accordance with this belief, and he derives the Word of the Lord from the Gospels. The testimony of "the disciples of Jesus and of the Apostles" (*vide* chap. iv. 5, etc.) occupies only a secondary place in his regard; for him it has clearly no independent, but only a derivative, authority (as it, and so far as it coincides with the Words of the Saviour); he quotes only Epistles of St Paul and statements of John, the Apostle and Evangelist. Lastly, he takes account of the *ἀποστολικὴ παράδοσις, ἣν ἐκ διαδοχῆς καὶ ἡμεῖς παρειλήφαμεν* (chap. v. 10). Therefore in the case of Ptolemy we cannot speak of a New Testament, because he evidently does not possess or know of a collection in which Gospels and Apostolic Epistles stand on one level. All that we learn elsewhere of the ancient Valentinian School and of Valentinus himself fits in

[1] *τῶν ῥηθησομένων ἡμῖν τὰς ἀποδείξεις ἐκ τῶν τοῦ σωτῆρος ἡμῶν λόγων παριστῶντες, δι' ὧν μόνον ἔστιν ἀπταίστως ἐπὶ τὴν κατάληψιν τῶν ὄντων ὁδηγεῖσθαι.*

with what we learn from Ptolemy. Their high reverence for, and their use of the Pauline Epistles never justify the equation: "Epistulæ (*i.e.* Paulus)=Evangelia." I cannot see, as Zahn asserts, that "clear traces" of the Acts, 1 and 2 Peter, and Hebrews are to be found among the Valentinians; but even if that were so, there would still remain the question what value Valentinus and his school ascribed to these works. Summing up, we may say that Valentinus and his earlier followers set up in place of the Old Testament as their highest court of appeal the Word of the Lord contained in the Gospels, with which they associated, as a secondary authority, the Pauline Epistles and their own secret Apostolic tradition. Among them nothing like the New Testament, so far as structure is concerned, was as yet in existence. Arguing, then, from this to what then obtained in the Church, we can only say: The Church at that time possessed the Canon of the Four Gospels, and read side by side with it the collection of Pauline Epistles. This, however, does not carry us very far in Zahn's direction.

3. According to Zahn, Justin is a witness to the New Testament for (*a*) he places the Ἀπομνημονεύματα τῶν ἀποστόλων on the same level with the "Writings of the Prophets"; "as, however, the whole Old Testament is intended to be included under the latter title, *so also the name* Ἀπομν. τ. ἀποστ. *by no means excludes other Christian writings*"; (*b*) Justin knows the Johannine Apocalypse as a work of the Apostle John and as a genuine product of Christian Prophecy;[1] (*c*) "Justin as an apologist had no occasion to mention other

[1] Zahn adds (p. 34): "It is self-evident that the Apocalypse, in accordance with its own demand, was repeatedly read aloud in the assemblies of the communities that so accepted it."

Apostolic works in the same way as the Apocalypse; but we find that his religious ideas and form of expression are affected by his diligent reading, of the following works: Rom., 1 Cor., Gal., Eph., (Phil. ?), Col., 2 Thess., (Titus, 1 Tim. ?), Heb., 1 Pet., (James ?), Acts, and Didache." Against these statements we would assert that (α) the statement that the expression Ἀπομν. τ. ἀποστ. does not exclude other Christian writings is only correct if we at once add *that it also does not include them.* I will not waste words here, for the thesis is as inadmissible as the argument by which it is based on the clause, "The whole Old Testament is intended to be included under the Writings of the Prophets." Are then Συγγράμματα and Ἀπομνημονεύματα the same? Can we subsume the Pauline Epistles or the Acts of the Apostles under Ἀπομνημονεύματα? (β) The fact that Justin knows of the Apocalypse and knows of it as a book of public lection—though, indeed, he does say this in so many words—has nothing to do with the question of the New Testament so long as we do not know whether this book was placed on a level with the *Gospels* at the time of Justin. If the Apocalypse stood by itself, like many other Jewish and Christian Apocalypses at that time, Justin's notice does not come into consideration for the history of the New Testament in the strict sense of the term. (γ) Justin's views and expressions may have been influenced by many early Christian writings, traces of which Zahn believes that he has found; yet Zahn himself does not venture to assert that Justin regarded these as canonical; Zahn leaves this conclusion to the reader. However, a reader who carefully studies the Dialogue with Trypho is not only not able to draw such a conclusion, but is rather compelled to regard the opposite as proved. Zahn, indeed, asserts that Justin, as an apologist, had no occasion to express himself concerning the canonical prestige of Apostolic works; but the case is otherwise: Justin, with an enormous expense of labour in collection of passages, seeks to deduce a New Testament (or the New Testament) from the Old Testament, and from the Old Testament to prove its existence. He could not do otherwise in controversy with a Jew. But why does he not do what, for instance, Tertullian does dozens of times in reference to the Collection of Sayings of the Paraclete, which was not recognised by his opponents in the Church? Why does he not *once* at least say: "We Christians possess a New Testament in form of litera scripta"? The reserve which he here adopts is simply unintelligible if a New Testament was in existence in the Church. It was simply not in existence! *Justin knows the new Covenant as a fact that had its litera scripta only in the Old Testament.* He says nothing about the New Testament, not only because he is an apologist, but because no New Testament stood at his disposal; he never speaks even of the Gospels as "New Testament," and if he had done so there is nothing to show that for Justin other early Christian writings stood upon the same high level as the Gospels. The grounds for the assertion that Justin presupposes the New Testament are as unsound as in the cases of Marcion and Valentinus.

Lastly, in the section dealing with the New Testament of about A.D. 170–220, Zahn investigates the changes that the already existing New Testament experienced during that period. Here, however, as a kind of headline, we find the sentence (p. 15): "The New Testament at that time was far from being something clearly defined." In fact as we read the many detailed discussions here and in the parallel sections of the larger work, we not seldom forget that we are supposed to be dealing with certain discrepancies in a work already created; rather we have the impression that we have before us *something that is just coming into being.* Hence there is comparatively little here that provokes controversy, and, indeed, it may be regarded a matter of indifference whether we describe the tremendous changes, which Zahn himself allows to have taken place between A.D. 170 and 220, as the "Origin" of the New Testament out of previous stages of existence, or as the "development" of something that was already in existence, but was as yet unborn. Zahn himself, however, allows, so far as I see, that the name "New Testament" first makes its appearance during this period.

Zahn himself will not have us speak in set words of the "New Testament" until about A.D. 130 or 140; he asserts its existence for the following generation (even if the name is absent); but on the one hand the proofs for the latter thesis do not hold good, and on the other hand he himself allows that the New Testament about A.D. 170 was still an unfinished work, and in any case that *nowhere in the Church* did it appear as something clearly defined. There is no question, therefore, of a difference of one hundred years between Zahn and the other critics, but of a much smaller space of time, which would contract still more closely if Zahn would bring himself to take as *punctum saliens* not the public lection of the separate works, but the setting of a new collection of sacred writings on a level with the Old Testament.

With these remarks I am far from wishing to renew

a controversy that years ago was carried on between Zahn and myself with only too much strong feeling; but seeing that an accurate and scientifically balanced account of the character of the controversy has not been drawn up, and seeing especially that the actual results of Zahn's work are exploited in favour of an entirely unscientific point of view, it seemed to me necessary, in these studies of the origin of the New Testament, to set the facts in a clear light.

PRINTED IN GREAT BRITAIN BY NEILL AND CO., LTD., EDINBURGH.